PLAIN
TALK
ON
the Minor Prophets

PLAIN
TALK
ON
the Minor Prophets

MANFORD GEORGE GUTZKE
PH.D.

ZONDERVAN
PUBLISHING HOUSE

OF THE ZONDERVAN CORPORATION
GRAND RAPIDS, MICHIGAN 49506

PLAIN TALK ON THE MINOR PROPHETS
Copyright © 1980 by The Zondervan Corporation

Second printing 1982

Library of Congress Cataloging in Publication Data

Gutzke, Manford George.
    Plain talk on the Minor prophets.

    1. Bible. O.T. Minor prophets—Criticism, interpretation, etc. I. Title.
BS1560.G87   224'.906   80-20041
ISBN 0-310-41941-7

Printed in the United States of America

Contents

HOSEA

† † †

WHEN WE THINK about the Minor Prophets, we should note that the term *minor* has been added by Bible students. The Bible never speaks of Joel as a "minor prophet." Or Amos. Or Malachi. Persons who read and study the Bible have done that. The term *minor* simply means that these books are shorter in length than the "major prophets." The prophets of whatever label were the preachers of the Old Testament.

When the Creator of the heavens and the earth made man, He made a creature in His own image. This creature had opportunities, capacities, and responsibilities that no other creature of God has. He was placed at the top of God's creation. God put man in charge of everything. Man was to have dominion over the earth and to control it, being responsible to God.

But man had in him certain desires of his own for things that were not good for him. Because he wanted them, he took them and so injured himself. The biblical record is that man sinned and because of sin he was to die. The prospect of death and destruction brings distress. Any number of people live all their days under the pall, the unhappy expectation, that when they are through living they will be destroyed. They are often

in a mess now; they try to keep their neighbors from finding
that out. But it eventually shows up. Before they are finished
they will come to death.

There is another aspect of man that we should note at this
point. Man has the capacity of loving. He can become affec-
tionate about certain specific objects, certain persons. Parents
love their children; families love each other. Love does not
want separation; love does not want ruin; love does not want
destruction. Love's greatest enemy is death. And because of
this man can experience pathetic lasting sorrow and grief.
"Change and decay in all around I see" goes the hymn "Abide
With Me." That is the truth. God is compassionate and looks
down upon mankind with pity and with mercy. God so loved
the world—this doomed world heading into destruction—
that He gave His only begotten Son, so that whoever believes
in Him should not perish but have everlasting life. He offers
to mankind a promise. We know the promise very well, but
let us think it over again: "Come unto me, all ye that labor and
are heavy laden, and I will give you rest" (Matt. 11:28). You
worn out weary ones, come to me; I will give you rest. I will
give you relief. I will save you.

God calls to Himself everybody, "whosoever will." Anyone
who will come to Him and trust His promises will be saved
from the condition he is in. He will be saved from the fate that
he is facing. He will be saved from the world; God will call
him out of it. The very word for "church"—*ekklesia* in the
Greek—means "the called out ones." These people are those
who are believers in this promise of God. They have forsaken
their natural condition and are moved into a new relationship.
These are called the people of God. In Old Testament times
that was Israel; in our day and time this is the church.

God has called. He calls everyone. The Scriptures tell us
that God is not willing that any should perish but that all
should come to repentance (2 Peter 3:9). When a person hears
the promise of God, he takes it to his heart and he believes it.
It works in him. He becomes one of His people. Anyone can
have this relationship who wishes it. Anyone who claims the
promise has it. The taking of it and the having of it are by
faith.

But faith is something that varies. It can be stronger; it can be weaker. It has to be fed. Faith does not lie in our own strength. Someone will object that faith is given to us by the Holy Spirit. I know that faith is given to us by the Holy Spirit, as our life is given to us by God; but we have to eat to live. Life is given to us as a gift, but we must eat to keep ourselves alive. In the same way, faith is given to us, but we have to feed our faith.

The feeding of faith is by the Word of God, which is the Bread of Life. The soul feeds on the Word of God. It is the work of God in the soul that will cause a person to be regenerated and born again, but the new life's faith must be fed. "As newborn babes, desire the sincere milk of the word, that ye may grow thereby" (1 Peter 2:2). The soul must be fed. And it is here that believers have something to do. The feeding of souls is done by someone who has it in hand to feed them— such as apostles, pastors, evangelists. In Old Testament times there were the prophets. The prophet was the feeder of the people; he fed their souls with the Word of God.

As we read the Book of Hosea, especially the first three chapters, we find out that there was a man named Hosea with whom God dealt in a special way. It is a shocking thing that to this day some people read this book and do not believe it, because of what Hosea did. We will consider his actions in a moment. But the record shows that God led Hosea through a certain experience for a purpose. As Hosea passed through this certain experience, God gave Hosea to understand this would be the way He would deal with His people. We find out as we read Hosea that God is speaking to His people through this book and this messenger.

As we read other minor prophets such as Amos, we find again that God has His people in mind. Amos was God's spokesman. Amos talked for God to the people and explained to them the meaning of their own experience. He told them what was happening to them. He reminded them of God's promise, reminded them of their relationship with God, and warned them that they could not be careless with God. God has ways of integrity, and He wants His people to follow His will.

Amos showed the people that if they would be willing to

repent, confess their sins, forsake their sins, and turn to God, God would bless them. But if they would not do that, God would chasten them.

In Joel we find the same truth. And in Micah. Certain other prophets preached to other nations. This reveals something of the function of the prophets as it is recorded in the history of the Old Testament.

ISRAEL AND THE CHURCH

This reference to history may make it appropriate to compare Israel and the church. In reading about Israel, we may note that the prophets dealt a great deal with political circumstances, moral conduct, and social injustices. Some people today believe that in this there lies a cue for all preachers in the church to preach on the social injustices of the day.

It should be remembered that the prophets were dealing with God's people at that time. They were telling God's people about how, in the day of Israel, the blessings of God were manifested to God's people in external things. For instance, if the people were favored of God, it would rain on their crops. If they were obedient to God, there would not be insects and pests to ruin their crops. If they were obedient to God, they would have military victory over their enemies. That was for God's people back in Israel's day by way of illustrating eternal truth. In our day and time, such is not the case.

God is not interested in setting up a particular economic system in the world. What God is primarily interested in is having His people understand how to yield themselves to Him, to let Him work in them. The blessings that believers experience today are not equated with good crops, lots of olives on the olive trees, plenty of fruit in the orchards, plenty of sheep, plenty of cattle. That is not the nature of blessing upon believers in Christ. Rain on the crops is not a special blessing today. It falls on both "the just and the unjust." It is what we call a temporal blessing.

Spiritual blessings are love, peace, joy, inward comfort, inward relief from passion, inward victory over evil, quietness, confidence, fellowship with God, an assurance of the life in the world to come, an inward strength to walk with God. Such are the blessings that belong to believers in Christ alone. A person is blessed of God when his faith is strong, his hope is sure, his love is abounding. The grace in the heart of a believer in Christ overcomes all the evil he faces.

If others do not treat him right, he could perhaps give them what they gave him, and that would mean trouble. He might even feel like doing it. But there is a new thing in him: they deserve that kind of treatment, but he no longer acts on that level; he is now a child of God. He belongs to God, and because God dealt graciously with him, he will deal graciously with others. That person who has annoyed the believer in Christ, irritated him, or harmed him deserves to be punished. But the believer once deserved to be punished by God. Instead God manifested to him grace and forgave him what he did wrong. Now the believer in turn manifests grace and forgives the offending person.

When a person is blessed, he has inwardly the grace in his heart to believe the promise of God. He really believes he is a child of God because God said so. He is confident that the Holy Spirit is actually in him. He cannot put his finger on it, cannot even feel it. The Holy Spirit is not something— Someone—that he can sense as if it were a fragrance or a wind blowing or anything like that. It is not physical. But it is just as real as he is—it is the presence of God.

The believer in Christ has it in his heart to believe in the presence of God. He believes in the promises of God. He believes that God is; he believes that the Lord Jesus Christ is at the right hand of God, praying for him. He thinks this is real now. As he goes on about his work each day he has an inward quietness and comfort that will be his strength. The blessing of God is the peace of mind, the quietness of heart, and the good will he has toward others when they do not deserve it: he wishes them well.

When the believer in Christ understands this spiritually, he knows that it is the grace of God in his heart. He thanks God for it. He feels good toward others. As the song goes, the old-time religion makes him love everybody. It fills his heart with joy. He looks for God's presence, and he knows that God is with him. Even when the day of separation comes, when bereavement comes to his family and he must let some loved one go, an amazing thing happens: the reality of the presence of God becomes for him a sweet thing. The people of the world cannot understand it.

In Israel's day the blessing of God was interpreted in such things as good crops, good success in business, protection from enemies, victory over the Assyrians, and the like. Those were the temporal blessings of that time. It is very confusing to bring such things over into our time and to say today that in the prophets we have a message to the White House or a message to the Kremlin in Moscow. Such interpretation brings great confusion when preachers try to be international politicians and give advice to the government on technical affairs in various matters. We will not understand the prophets if we think in that way. We should understand them as preachers. The prophets were preaching to God's people about God's promises.

Prophets are to be counted like preachers, and all preachers are to be counted as messengers from God. Whenever a preacher faces a group of human beings, he is bound to appreciate the fact that they have problems. In these problems they could benefit from good advice as to what they should do. The preacher may have in his heart and mind that he knows what good advice to give them, and he may give it out on the side. But he has not yet started preaching. He cannot start preaching until he personally becomes aware of the revelation of God's will. What would God do about that situation? What promise does God give to people about their problems? The preacher, understanding the people, knowing the situation, understanding something of the Word of God, and knowing something of the mind of God, puts it all together; opening the mind of the people, he gives them the Word of God. He will point out not what they should do, but what God will do for them if they put their trust in Him. That is preaching.

A preacher tells us what God's plan is and how God works, so that the people listening can see. Then it is up to us to decide whether we want to commit ourselves to God. By his analysis of our problems and his teaching and expounding the

Word of God, the preacher can show us that in the Scriptures our situation has actually been set forth, and such and such is God's way of working in just such a situation. Thus God worked with Abraham. Thus He worked with Moses. Thus He worked with Daniel. Thus He worked with Paul. Thus He worked with Peter. Thus He will work with us. So we, listening, get the idea of what God promises to do, and we are challenged to believe it. Believing it means we will yield to it. We say, "Even so, Lord, do it unto me." We commit ourselves to God. That is the consequence of preaching.

Preachers are to be ministers of the Word of God. It is the preacher's business; it was the prophets' business. The prophets came to God's people to show them God's will. After we have understood that God will bless us if we will put our trust in Him, we may believe in God that He will bless us, and we may commit ourselves to Him in something that is very much like getting married. We may actually commit ourselves to God and let Him work in us; but, being human beings, we may forget.

It can happen that a man will marry a woman expecting that from then on, he will never be out of her sight, nor she out of his. It would be his great pleasure if they never had one time to be out of each other's sight. When he went to work in the morning she would feel bad, and when he came home at night he would feel very good. But we know what can happen. It can happen that he will neglect or forget those feelings. He may go to work and then go on to something else for a while. When he does return, it may be a long time later. She may have waited in vain for him. Or she may go, and he may wait in vain for her. These things happen to human beings.

Such things happen to people believing in God. The heart may get cool, the faith weak. Some people may wander away. But God, being a partner in this communion and fellowship, does not let it happen without doing something about it. He acts like a parent with a child. A child can forget who is boss. A child can forget who is running the place. The child may even start a little war to resolve the issue one more time. God's people sometimes have such experiences, too, and God's way of dealing with His people is to be seen in Scripture.

God deals with people in two ways. In one structure of

relationship, God deals with people according to the laws of nature. And in the laws of nature, this is the principle that prevails: "Whatsoever a man soweth, that shall he also reap." A person gets what he earns. In this relationship the emphasis is upon works. What the person does, he cashes in on. For example, in regard to personal virtue, if he is good he will be blessed; if he is evil he will be cursed. All human beings are normally and naturally born into this world, so that all stand in a natural relationship with God. God is in control over them all. They live in nature and so they are under law. In this natural situation, people are lost. They are ruined. "All our righteousness is as filthy rags" in the presence of God.

On the basis of the natural way of doing things, people get what they deserve. Naturally people are lost. Such persons have sinned; and the sinner shall die. That is their natural end. Human beings always live in the apprehension of future judgment and destruction. Many realize this with resentment. In their reaction to that consciousness, there is a natural resentment against God. They are angry with Him and consider Him unfair: He is not doing right by them. They feel their lot is terrible. But these feelings are various ways of alibiing their own responsibility for the situation. "The carnal mind is enmity against God: for it is not subject to the law of God, neither indeed can be" (Rom. 8:7). The reason why the natural person is an enemy of God is because he is guilty and is facing destruction. No one wants to be destroyed. We have never yet seen a case of a prisoner condemned to the dock who loved the judge. This does not happen.

But God works another way in another structure of relationships. Having called the first one "nature," the other one we call "grace." God's way of dealing with people in Christ Jesus is by grace, in which mercy and kindness and the grace of God prevail. The main principle in the grace relationship is that the believer in Christ gets what God gives him. He does not receive what he deserves—destruction. He receives what God gives him—eternal life. He receives freedom. He receives forgiveness. He receives all these things from God.

In this second way of living, in this structure of grace relationship, the emphasis is upon faith. In the first one the emphasis is upon works: whatever the person does, he will

receive in kind. But in the second one the emphasis is upon
faith: he receives and takes. What God wants to give him, he
will have. Here the emphasis is on the faith of man and the
grace of God. All who obey the word receive the promise.
Those who believe in God are in this structure of grace in the
Holy Spirit. In this setting, the believer in Christ is saved,
just as in the other setting, natural man is ruined and lost.

A man is born the first time into nature, without his consent.
But the believer in Christ is born the second time in spirit, only
with his consent. In this second relationship, in which God is
going to give His blessing, the believer must agree to receive
it. God will not push it on anyone. Spiritual relationship is
basically one of communion, and it is effective in love and by
love and through love. But when *love* is used in the New
Testament, it is not referring just to an inward sentiment.

Love is something a person does. Love is a very practical
thing. When the Scriptures say "God so loved the world," it
does not mean "God so *liked* the world" that He gave. The
world lies in the lap of the evil one. God is angry with the
wicked every day. The sinfulness of man hurts God's heart.
God does not *like* the world. God does not *like* sinners. He
loves them. "God so loved the world that He gave His only
begotten Son." Love is a word of action. It is something we
do. In love we do *to* and *for* another. That is loving. In that
way we can love *anyone*. We can do for someone. That is the
only way we can love our enemy.

We cannot be normal and like the person who is trying to
hurt us. To like such a person, we would have to be morbid or
psychopathic. But we can love them. What does it mean to
"love the enemy"? Marry him? Not necessarily. In loving
them we help them if we can.

The first of the minor prophets to draw our attention was
very much a person characterized by love and the grace relationship.

PREACHING TO GOD'S PEOPLE

Hosea is one of many examples of how God used the prophets to illustrate vital truth. It is a common practice for preachers

to illustrate. They use object lessons. They gesture, do things to attract attention, and give parables to express truth. God directed His servants in the Old Testament, these prophets, on occasion to act in certain ways that were typical or symbolic of certain truth. He had them do specific things. In the story of Hosea, we read about a preacher who was sent to God's people to minister to them with a very important message.

Who are God's people? Human beings on earth related to God by faith. God's people in Hosea's time were Israel. And Israel was a people whom God had blessed. He had led them out of Egypt. He had led them into the Promised Land. He had put to flight their enemies. He had given them the control of the country, and had blessed them throughout the years. But Israel's heart was prone to turn away from God. By the time Hosea arrived on the scene, the people were prosperous. The temple was filled with worshipers. People brought sacrifices to the temple by the thousands. Lambs and oxen were killed, and their blood was shed. But while all these religious practices were going on, the people's hearts were far from God. Many were getting richer in material things by oppressing the poor. They were dissipating themselves by irresponsible living. They were immoral. They were traitors to their country. They were unfaithful. They were dishonest. Their homes were being broken up. This was their condition. Yes, they were rich; they had their big city of Jerusalem; they had the temple and religious services—big religious services. But they did not really worship. Their hearts were far from it. Their preachers—Isaiah, Amos, Micah, and the other prophets—told the people, "God isn't fooled a single bit by what you do. If you do not mean it, He would rather you would not do it."

Hosea put his finger on something specific when he preached. He explained to the people what was wrong. He went to the bottom of the whole situation, pointing out what was wrong with them and what God would do.

While Hosea was a preacher, God told him to get married. This does not mean that Hosea had not thought about marriage, but it does mean that God gave him liberty and guidance in the matter. God said to Hosea, "Go, take unto thee a wife of whoredoms and children of whoredoms."

Scholars have some difference of opinion as to whether Hosea's wife was an unfaithful and immoral woman before he married her or whether she just lived in an unfaithful, immoral society and would eventually become immoral. I am inclined to think God said to Hosea, "Marry one of the women of the age in which you live." It would be much like someone years ago saying to a young ministerial candidate, "Marry one of these flappers and be done with it." It would not necessarily mean that the girl had done something wrong up to that time, but rather that she lived in a wayward society.

Hosea, a godly man and a servant of God, married a woman named Gomer who was chosen by God. He had several children with her. Then she became involved with other men. The record seems to support the idea that she somehow felt Hosea was not giving her the benefits that she had before. She felt that she was actually getting more from other people than she was getting from her husband. As she became involved with other men, she became immoral and ran away from home.

This is not different from tragedies that happen even in our day, and as such it is hardly significant enough to relate in the Bible. But there is more to Gomer's story. When she had lived a life of sin over a length of time, everyone knew who she was and knew where to find her. Her presence and her person could be bought; the language implies that she could be bought like a slave. She would contract herself to live with any man for so much money. All would recognize that as being a harlot's hire. Anyone from any country would know she was a prostitute.

There came a day when Gomer lost her beauty. Nobody wanted her. So she was on "the open market" for anyone who would hire her or buy her; and nobody would. Now she had no money; she was rejected and an outcast; and nobody wanted her.

Hosea hired Gomer like a harlot, took her home, and reinstated her as his wife. That is the record in the Book of Hosea. Hosea took this woman: he cleaned her up, brought her back into his home, and made her his wife, restoring her to her former place. Everyone knew it and was shocked. But Hosea preached, "What you saw me do with my wife is what

God will do with you. You are just like she was. God called you to Himself when you were young. God took you to Himself when you were weak. When you were nothing, God made you His bride and gave you blessings. He surrounded you with His favors. He watched over you and kept you. But your heart was not true. You went off to other gods. You began to think that the people from the east had more knowledge than your prophets had. You looked into other religions, and you became enamored with other things."

The gospel truth revealed in the Book of Hosea is that after men have gone after other gods, after they have given their hearts over to worldly things, after they have entered into things that dissipate and ruin the soul until they are lost, after they have grown weak and ungodly, then God sends His Son to die for them. Jesus Christ died on a cross to "redeem" lost people—to "buy them back" from slavery to sin and to restore them to a wholesome relationship with God. In this "God commendeth his love toward us, in that, while we were yet sinners, Christ died for us" (Rom. 5:8). This amazing truth is that God would come for us when we were away from Him, knowing that we had willfully turned away from Him.

So great was the love of God toward Israel that He sent Hosea after these people to tell them "God will let you suffer for the wrong you have done, when you forsook Him. Sin will run its course. You will go with these men who have hired you until they strip you, until they leave you naked, until they forsake you, until you are utterly worthless; and then when you do not have a thing left, and all your natural beauty is gone, and all your natural attractiveness has been ruined, then God will show you what He will do. God will take you back."

Just think what a powerful preacher Hosea was, preaching out of a heart that had experienced what he had! He preached to those people the everlasting, marvelous, wonderful love of God that does not pass away. God's love was so great that the people's unfaithfulness could not quench it.

In Hosea we can understand this word: "I am God, not man." If Hosea had acted like man, he would have let his wife go. But see what God says: "I am not a man." It is as simple as this: it belongs to God to forgive sin. Yet it is as profound as the deepest evil a man can do: to forgive sin. We should not think this does not hurt God. It cost Him His own Son. We should never think that sin does not grieve God: it breaks His heart. But God being God, having given Himself, He will not take Himself back from us. In Hosea is the word, "I have loved thee with an everlasting love." God's love toward His people is not on any teeter-totter basis: "I love you, then you love me, then I love you and then you love me; but if you do not love me then I will not love you." No. It is "I love you. I love you. Every morning, every noon, every night, every day I love you, I love you. When you do well, I love you—I am happy. When you do evil, I love you—I grieve. I love you. It does not mean I like you. It means I will give myself for you." In the Book of Hosea we see this preacher, in his integrity, taking himself in the community, taking himself in that home, reinstating in that place his wife, and then facing the public. They all knew her. But now they knew Hosea as they had never known him before.

As we read through the Book of Hosea we will find so many things that God has to say pointing out to Hosea the coldness of heart that caused this spiritual unfaithfulness. They are hidden things and cannot be seen openly. People can come to church and can participate in worship services while their hearts are far from God. Only God knows it, but God does know it. He showed Hosea just how He felt about this sin.

> Hear the word of the Lord, ye children of Israel: for the Lord hath a controversy with the inhabitants of the land, because there is no truth, nor mercy, nor knowledge of God in the land. . . . My people are destroyed for lack of knowledge: because thou hast rejected knowledge, I will also reject thee, that thou shalt be no priest to me: seeing thou hast forgotten the law of thy God, I will also forget thy children (Hosea 4:1, 6).

> My people ask counsel at their stocks (Hosea 4:12).

The word "stocks" refers to certain wooden idols. "Ask counsel" means that the people get their advice and guidance from natural ideas. There were natural interpretations of life and natural principles that the pagans were following. They interpreted things contradictory to the prophets of God. Israel took advice from these idolatrous ideas:

> . . . and their staff declareth unto them: for the spirit of
> whoredoms hath caused them to err, and they have gone a
> whoring from under their God (Hosea 4:12).

This unpleasant word, this inelegant word "whoredoms," implies the spiritual interests of the heart being given over to
something else than to God.

Chapter 5 of Hosea draws attention to the fact that it was
the priests who were at fault. They were the leaders.

> Hear ye this, O priests; and hearken, ye house of Israel; and
> give ye ear, O house of the king; for judgment is toward you,
> because ye have been a snare on Mizpah, and a net spread
> upon Tabor (Hosea 5:1).

This language is rather obscure and unfamiliar to us, but it
would seem that the prophet is accusing the priests and the
leaders. He is blaming the leaders for the unfaithfulness of the
people. The last verse in chapter 5 indicates God is speaking:

> I will go and return to my place, till they acknowledge their
> offense, and seek my face: in their affliction they will seek me
> early (Hosea 5:15).

This verse means to say, "I will withdraw myself from them
and let them go until they get into real trouble."

Then in chapter 6 comes the people's response:

> Come, and let us return unto the Lord: for he hath torn, and he
> will heal us; he hath smitten, and he will bind us up. After two
> days will he revive us: in the third day he will raise us up, and
> we shall live in his sight. Then shall we know, if we follow on to
> know the Lord: his going forth is prepared as the morning; and
> he shall come unto us as the rain, as the latter and former rain
> unto the earth (Hosea 6:1-3).

This is the response of repentance. But the underlying thrust
of Hosea's preaching is the great thing we have already talked
about. Hosea is called "the St. John of the Old Testament":
what John the apostle was to the New Testament in his writing, Hosea is to the Old Testament in his writing. John is
noted because he refers to love so often and describes the love
of God. Hosea is the outstanding prophet of the love of God in
the Old Testament and was used, as we have noted, to illustrate personally the marvelous love of God toward His people.

We do not know how the heart can ever fully grasp the

amazing love of God. Though we deny Him, yet He will not deny us. God, having begun a good work in us, will complete it. If ever any person turns his heart with sincerity to God and gives himself to Him, from then on his ultimate future does not depend upon his unbroken faithfulness—because he may stagger or stumble on occasion—but God who has begun a good work in him will complete it. God will not fail nor be discouraged. Believers in Christ are being loved with the everlasting love of almighty God.

JOEL

✝ ✝ ✝

AS WE CONSIDER the prophet Joel, let us give attention to a particular aspect of preaching. A preacher is one because of the people to whom he preaches and because of God's Word which he preaches. A preacher has a message that he did not invent. He did not put it together. A message was given to him to deliver. That message is not a secret message, because the Gospel is to be found in the Scriptures of the Old and New Testaments and has been set forth in the name and the person of the Lord Jesus Christ throughout the centuries. The Gospel is "good news." A minister of the Gospel is one who carries this message out to people.

The prophets in the Old Testament were preachers whose function related particularly to Israel. Israel were people related to God by faith. In the Old Testament days, before Jesus Christ lived, there were only the promises of God. The promises in the Old Testament set forth how God would bless His people. God promised Abraham that He would bless him, make him a blessing to others, and bless his seed. The children of Israel were included in that promise.

At the time when Joel and the other prophets lived, there were some people who had a special relationship with God. They were trusting in God to keep them, to bless them. They had promises for that. But as we clearly see set out in the course of the Scriptures, God's promises always involved the person's responding to them. It was not that the believer had to go and do something—as if deeds counted—rather, he had to *come* to do something. The believer was to come to the Lord trusting in Him according to His promise. The believer needed to let the Word of God function in him if he wanted the blessing of God on him. The road was before him. If he walked with the Lord, he would have His blessing. If he walked apart from Him, he would not.

But people, being as they are, need help. We need help to understand the ways of God. We need help to interpret what God's will really means for us. We need help to be encouraged to do the very things we know. We need help to be reminded of the things that we have learned. Such help came to Old Testament people through the prophets.

Joel is one of the minor prophets. We have practically no clue as to when he preached. The Book of Joel in itself, in its prophecy, is a message aimed directly into spiritual matters. It would appear from what we read that there had been some combination of great calamities in the country. The people were agricultural, depending largely on the crops and the cattle for their food and their economy. The calamity or calamities Joel refers to were so notable they would be talked about for three generations.

> Tell ye your children of it, and let your children tell their children, and their children another generation. That which the palmerworm hath left hath the locust eaten; and that which the locust hath left hath the cankerworm eaten; and that which the cankerworm hath left hath the caterpillar eaten (Joel 1:3-4).

These particular insects and pests may not specifically affect us today, but he is saying that the people of Israel had four successive plagues because of them.

Later in this same chapter is mentioned another calamity—drought. Calamities such as pestilence and drought go together.

> The vine is dried up, and the fig tree languisheth; the pomegranate tree, the palm tree also, and the apple tree, even all the trees of the field, are withered: because joy is withered away from the sons of men (Joel 1:12).

In a country depending on the crops of the soil, these calamities can devastate a community. Joel makes this setting the start of his message. What would have been a typical natural calamity for anyone else was not a typical natural calamity for Israel, because Israel had a promise from God to cover these things. When they had such calamities and plagues, Joel the preacher immediately pointed out that this was evidence that God had withdrawn His favor.

When God withdrew His favor from His people, it was always the time to ask why. The promises in Old Testament times dealing with temporal matters and this world's goods are examples, illustrations, and types of the kind of promises you and I have. What are our promises? Peace of mind. Joy in our hearts. Strength in our faith. Good will among friends. Love in the family. These are the blessings that God gives to us His people.

Joel the preacher took note of the fact that natural calamities had beset the country and had impoverished them all. He called upon Israel to do what any preacher would call upon God's people to do when they are in trouble: turn to God. If God is withholding His blessing, look up into His face. The believer has no other recourse; there is no point in going anywhere else. So Joel admonished the people, "Do not let this calamity just go on this way. Do not let this evidence of the lack of blessing just fall to the ground. If God is withholding His blessing, there is a reason. Come into the presence of God and face Him."

Joel was doing the work of a preacher when he called on his people to turn and face God.

> Gird yourselves, and lament, ye priests: howl, ye ministers of the altar: come, lie all night in sackcloth, ye ministers of my God: for the meat offering and the drink offering is withholden from the house of your God (Joel 1:13).

Joel called upon the leaders, the preachers, the elders, the church officers to humble themselves before God and seek God's face. What we need to learn from this is that if we have the feeling there is something wrong in our spiritual life, if things are getting dry and barren, then this is the time to call upon ourselves to face God. We need to come into His presence.

Notice the language here: "Gird yourselves, and lament, ye priests." What does Joel mean by "lament"? He means to look at the facts, admit that they are as bad as they are, and tell the truth about them. They will make you cry? Well then, cry. Be honest before God about it. "Howl, ye ministers of the altar." To "howl" is a distinctive Hebrew expression. We may not take it literally, but what it actually means is to admit the truth about this thing and feel just as bad as it looks. If in our church, the pastor calls a prayer meeting and hardly anyone comes, then we should cry out to the Lord about that. There is a reason why no one is coming. We should not pass over a thing like that.

> Sanctify ye a fast, call a solemn assembly, gather the elders and all the inhabitants of the land into the house of the Lord your God, and cry unto the Lord (Joel 1:14).

When we are not being blessed, we should notice it as a symptom. We know God wants to bless us. If we are not being blessed, we should say, "Wait, why am I not being blessed? Why are things being so empty with me?" If it is like that, there is something wrong. If something is wrong, we should turn right to God. As we go along in this study I hope we will recognize that these people, God's people, never in the wide world ever had the idea in mind that we have to be good first and then come to God. That is not the way the Bible puts it. We have to be hungry and then come. We have to be brokenhearted and then come. We have to be thirsty and then come. There is no better preparation in the world to come to God than to feel His need. And when we feel the need—"I am weak"—then come to God. "I am helpless"— then come to God. "I am worried"—then turn to God. "I am frightened"—then turn to God. All these are evidences of lack of strength; then God has not been with you. Since God is your Savior, turn to God. That is what Joel called upon the people of Israel to do.

> Alas for the day! for the day of the Lord is at hand, and as a destruction from the Almighty shall it come (Joel 1:15).

In Joel, one concept comes out very strongly: "The day of the Lord." Many people have wondered about this expression and the meaning of that concept. I am quite sure that the day of the Lord is not one twenty-four-hour period. The day of the Lord is not one split-second of an event. The day of the Lord is a period in which God takes over. The day of the Lord is a time when He moves in to handle the situation. It is as though I have been going along with my work and my life up to a certain point; and at that point God moves in to take over.

When God moves in to take over with His people, the first thing He does is judge them for their sins. That is what they were feeling when Joel was preaching. God's judgment for their sin was showing up in these calamities. As they began to wait on God, when they came to fast before Him, to look up into His face, and find out why their troubles were coming in upon them, then the great truth came to them: God was starting to work.

When we pray to God to do something for someone, do not try to hold back God's hand when He begins to move. It may be that this calamity—which may really be providential, but which leaves us feeling terrible—may be the only way in which God can begin to work to actually get anything done with us. Joel told the people, "The day of the Lord is at hand." The very calamities that we see show that God is beginning to work.

Do we realize what would happen if God blessed us when we were wayward in heart and failed to turn to Him honestly and sincerely—if despite all this, our homes, our families, our hearts, and our churches should be blessed? We would never come to God; we would get further and further and further away from Him. But God is too faithful to let that happen.

So let us learn this lesson from Joel: when troubles and distress come, let us ask ourselves, Is it possible that God is beginning to work in our souls? Is beginning to work in our family? When calamity comes into our lives, when any kind of distress or misfortune may come upon us, we should have in mind that God is operating and working in our lives.

The second chapter of the Book of Joel points out that the day of the Lord is great and terrible, and it asks, Who can abide it? In other words, this aspect of God's working may show up in our personal affairs and take the form of some sorrow or some distress—something to arouse us and turn us to Him. Joel brought this out in the second phase of his message.

> Therefore also now, saith the Lord, turn ye even to me with all your heart, and with fasting, and with weeping, and with mourning: and rend your heart, and not your garments, and turn unto the Lord your God: for he is gracious and merciful, slow to anger, and of great kindness, and repenteth him of the evil (Joel 2:12-13).

This teaches us that if we are upset because of the way things have gone and we feel personally that there is evidence of lack of blessing upon us, then we should turn to God and call upon Him. We can keep one thing in mind: God is merciful and gracious; He has great kindness. God is slow to anger.

> Who knoweth if he will return and repent, and leave a blessing behind him; even a meat offering and a drink offering unto the Lord your God? (Joel 2:14).

Joel then went on to say:

> Blow the trumpet in Zion, sanctify a fast, call a solemn assembly (Joel 2:15).

This is like saying, "Have a special series of services. Put on revival services in your church. Call your people back to God."

> Gather the people, sanctify the congregation, assemble the elders, gather the children, and those that suck the breasts: let the bridegroom go forth of his chamber, and the bride out of her closet. Let the priests, the ministers of the Lord, weep between the porch and the altar, and let them say, Spare thy people, O Lord, and give not thine heritage to reproach, that the heathen should rule over them: wherefore should they say among the people, Where is their God? (Joel 2:16-17).

Joel said to call all the people together to really seek God's face, and then let the preachers and the elders, the officers of the church, lead the people in confessing their own shortcomings before God. This was a great call to repentance. The course of this whole movement of thought in this book would indicate that God was not blessing His people. If God was not blessing, there must have been a reason. The reason must have resided in the people.

Joel called upon Israel to face God, to open their hearts before Him, to be honest with Him, and to recognize the truth of the matter. They should repent and call on God to be kind to them. God is merciful; He is kind. When all the people gathered together to seek God's face, the priests and the ministers of the Lord were to weep between the porch and the altar. These preachers, standing before God's people, were to lead them in humble contrition.

There is nothing in the world that disqualifies a person from further blessing more than cultivating complacency, with the feeling "We are doing all right. Everything is going just fine. We used to have 150 people at church, and now we have 175. We are steadily increasing. We used to have a budget of $10,000; now we have a budget of $12,000. We are just going along right up the road." This kind of thinking—this complacent way of looking at the situation, when all the time the evidence was that there was a lack of blessing of God—was not what Joel wanted.

Joel wanted the preachers and the leaders to weep before the temple. He wanted them to lead in praying, "Spare thy people, O Lord, and give not thine heritage to reproach, that the heathen should rule over them: wherefore should they say among the people, Where is their God?" Joel wanted the priests to be crying out to God and the ministers to be praying, "O God, be merciful to thy people. Don't let them be lost out there in this condition."

> Then will the Lord be jealous for his land, and pity his people.
> Yea, the Lord will answer and say unto his people, Behold, I
> will send you corn, and wine, and oil, and ye shall be satisfied
> therewith: and I will not more make you a reproach among the
> heathen: but I will remove far off from you the northern army,
> and will drive him into a land barren and desolate, with his face
> toward the east sea. . . . Fear not, O land; be glad and rejoice:
> for the Lord will do great things (Joel 2:18-21).

This was the word of promise that came. Apparently all that God was waiting for was a humble and contrite heart in His people. When this heart calls out to God for His blessing, then He will pour out His favor on Israel.

> Be glad then, ye children of Zion, and rejoice in the Lord your
> God: for he hath given you the former rain moderately, and he
> will cause to come down for you the rain, the former rain, and
> the latter rain in the first month. And the floors shall be full of
> wheat, and the vats shall overflow with wine and oil. And I will
> restore to you the years that the locust hath eaten, the canker-
> worm, and the caterpillar, and the palmerworm, my great

> army which I sent among you. And ye shall eat in plenty, and
> be satisfied, and praise the name of the Lord your God, that
> hath dealt wondrously with you: and my people shall never be
> ashamed. And ye shall know that I am in the midst of Israel,
> and that I am the Lord your God, and none else: and my
> people shall never be ashamed (Joel 2:23-27).

Isn't this wonderful? One promise after another of unending
favor from God. What qualified the people for them? A
genuine, sincere repentance and a contrite call upon God for
help. Humbling themselves and asking almighty God to be
kind to them meant that He who wanted to be kind would pour
out His blessing in the very places where He had withheld it.
There were crop failures, but now He will give crops abun-
dantly. There was drought, but now He will give plenty of rain.

This was also true spiritually. Where there was an inner
emptiness, now He would fill their hearts. Where there was a
coldness, now He would warm them. Where there was weakness, He would give them strength. Where there was uncertainty, He would give them assurance.

> And it shall come to pass afterward, that I will pour out my
> spirit upon all flesh; and your sons and your daughters shall
> prophesy, your old men shall dream dreams, your young men
> shall see visions: and also upon the servants and upon the
> handmaids in those days will I pour out my spirit (Joel 2:28-29).

Peter quoted this passage on the Day of Pentecost, saying,
"This is that which was spoken of by the prophet Joel." After
the people had been blessed, after their crops had been restored, after it had rained so that God's favor was expressed in
an outward, obvious way that they could understand—after
this, He Himself would come into them and change their
whole experience. He would come and live in them.

What does this mean for us? If we have reason to feel in
ourselves that God has withheld His favor, when we have
inward weakness, when we have inward uncertainty and
doubt, when we have the feeling that we have not been
blessed of God, then we must face God. When we realize we
have not been faithful and we have not really yielded to Him,
and then we throw ourselves upon His mercy and say, "God
be merciful to me a sinner," God will bless us. When we are
strong inside, it is a sign that He is blessing us and our

families. He will bless us among our friends and in our church. And in addition to all these evidences of blessing, His Spirit will come into our hearts and fill our hearts until the joy of the Lord is spread abroad. That is what He promised in the Book of Joel.

> And I will show wonders in the heavens and in the earth, blood, and fire, and pillars of smoke. The sun shall be turned into darkness, and the moon into blood, before the great and terrible day of the Lord come (Joel 2:30-31).

Before God is through, the whole powers of the world will be shaken. Every natural thing, as it were, will be shaken to its foundation.

> And it shall come to pass, that whosoever shall call on the name of the Lord shall be delivered: for in mount Zion and in Jerusalem shall be deliverance, as the Lord hath said, and in the remnant whom the Lord shall call (Joel 2:32).

In Old Testament times, this was pointing forward to something that would happen. And this was fulfilled in the time of Pentecost after the death and resurrection of the Lord Jesus Christ. At that time there was poured out into His church the Holy Spirit, who is operative to this day and who will work in believers in Christ in this same fashion. In chapter 3 of Joel we read that this is just the beginning of God's working. After He has blessed His people, God will then go on to call the whole world into judgment.

> For, behold, in those days, and in that time, when I shall bring again the captivity of Judah and Jerusalem, I will also gather all nations, and will bring them down into the valley of Jehoshaphat, and will plead with them there for my people and for my heritage Israel, whom they have scattered among the nations, and parted my land (Joel 3:1-2).

God revealed even more of His plan.

> Behold, I will raise them out of the place whither ye have sold them, and will return your recompense upon your own head: and I will sell your sons and your daughters into the hand of the children of Judah, and they shall sell them to the Sabeans, to a people far off: for the Lord hath spoken it (Joel 3:7-8).

God will visit judgment upon the whole world, especially any who have hindered and in any way hurt the Gospel of the Lord Jesus Christ in our day and time.

The final judgment will bring the people of the whole world together.

> Assemble yourselves, and come, all ye heathen, and gather yourselves together round about: thither cause thy mighty ones to come down, O Lord. Let the heathen be wakened, and come up to the valley of Jehoshaphat: for there will I sit to judge all the heathen round about. Put ye in the sickle, for the harvest is ripe. . . . Multitudes, multitudes in the valley of decision: for the day of the Lord is near in the valley of decision (Joel 3:11-14).

The natural universe will be broken up.

> The sun and the moon shall be darkened, and the stars shall withdraw their shining . . . But the Lord will be the hope of his people, and the strength of the children of Israel. So shall ye know that I am the Lord your God dwelling in Zion, my holy mountain: then shall Jerusalem be holy, and there shall no strangers pass through her any more (Joel 3:15-17).

This latter part of the prophecy of Joel seems to say that after God has brought His people back to Himself and has filled them with His Spirit, then He will deal with the world at large.

When God deals with the world, He deals with the people in judgment. He will bring them before Him at the harvest time, when He will bring judgment. This will be vindication of His people. When God so acts in judgment upon the whole world, it will be seen then that His people were wise when they put their trust in Him; and His people will know that He is the Lord their God.

> And it shall come to pass in that day, that the mountains shall drop down new wine, and the hills shall flow with milk, and all the rivers of Judah shall flow with waters, and a fountain shall come forth of the house of the Lord, and shall water the valley of Shittim. Egypt shall be a desolation, and Edom shall be a desolate wilderness, for the violence against the children of Judah, because they have shed innocent blood in their land (Joel 3:18-19).

When God brings His judgment upon the world, those forces that have been opposed to the Lord Jesus Christ and to the Gospel will suffer destruction.

> But Judah shall dwell for ever, and Jerusalem from generation to generation. For I will cleanse their blood that I have not cleansed: for the Lord dwelleth in Zion (Joel 3:20-21).

This is the great message of Joel. And this is the message of all the prophets. One reason why Joel is included in the prophets, I believe, even though there is no reference to any particular local historical incident, is that this is the general, eternal message of the prophets. Any prophetic preaching—that is to say, any interpreting of the Gospel of God to people—will come at it this way. This message was sent to God's own people, who had been wayward. Because the tendency of the human heart is to be wayward, it is also the tendency of the believer in Christ. The old nature in the believer will tend to turn him away from God.

Because the old man tends to turn away from God, God in mercy works in chastening. He lets trouble come to erring believers. Paul says that if we judge ourselves, we should not be judged; but if we do not judge ourselves, then are we chastened lest we be destroyed. God will not let us lose everything. If believers become wayward and careless, if they do not pay attention to God or cultivate their spiritual relationship with Him, then God will withdraw His favor just as soon as their hearts get cold. If any of us as believers in Christ find our hearts getting cold, we will find ourselves becoming uneasy. We will find ourselves becoming doubtful. We will find that we do not have blessing. Any of us who have ever tasted the good Word of God and know the power of the world to come will have a call within him, "Oh God, do not let this happen to me. It is not the way it was with me before. I do not feel good about these things." Then let us turn ourselves to God.

Joel would say just as surely as God has withdrawn His blessing, look up into His face. When we look up into the face of God we should be prepared to let the truth come out. We should tell the truth to God and confess to Him as we are and call upon God to bless us. God is merciful and kind and gracious and slow to anger and plenteous in mercy. We should trust Him. We should call upon Him, for we will find that God will come and bless us.

God will bless us by restoring the things that were taken away. If we have weakness, He will make us strong. If we have doubts, God will give us confidence. If we feel that everything is lost, God will give us assurance that nothing has been lost. And after God has given us this sense of rightness with Him, this reconciliation with Him, He will pour His Holy Spirit into our hearts. And when the Holy Spirit comes into our hearts, God will make us strong to be His witnesses. We will prophesy, as it were. We will witness elsewhere in the world.

And when that has happened with us, and we have come that way to God, God will then move out to judge others and everything else. The whole natural world will be judged as unfit for God. And in the course of that, when the world is brought into judgment, the world will be repudiated as far as God is concerned.

But we who put our trust in Him will be drawn nearer and nearer to Him, until finally we are absolutely convinced that the Lord our God is gracious and good. This is the message of Joel.

AMOS

† † †

THE BOOK OF AMOS is a series of messages brought to the people, and this makes it something special. God calls anybody and everybody to come and put their trust in Him. God is no respecter of persons. Whoever will may come. Some people will not come, and those who refuse do not enter into a relationship with Him. But others do come, and those who do so come to the Lord because they trust in Him. They are called God's people.

But people have a notable characteristic. At one time they may commit themselves to something—for instance, to God—and they mean to walk that way. They may be genuinely sincere. But people forget. Their resolutions can weaken. They can become so preoccupied with the daily round of duties that they can forget eternal things. Doubts will begin to rise and the darkness settles as the lights get dim. The light can get dim in the heart because men do not have it in themselves to believe. It is only as the truth of God is revealed to people that they have the ability to believe.

For this reason God has provided a special type of service. Certain persons are called to teach others and to remind us of the things of God. Some are called to preach. Preaching and teaching are very similar, yet they are a little different. There is a certain urgency in preaching. The prophets had a message to preach. It was not a message of their own making, for it had been revealed to them. There was something that God wanted His people to know and be reminded of. The prophets' mission was to bring these things to the attention of God's people. They were to remind the people. They were to reason with the people and to argue with them in their effort to get them to respond to the very things they already knew to be true about God.

Amos was given this task. He was to preach to a people who thought they knew God. They counted themselves God's people. These people, as history seems to imply, were practicing a certain kind of religion with reference to God. They had religious practices. They had a form of worship. They brought their sacrifices into the temple and performed their ritualistic exercises. But Amos was aware that while the people went through the motions of worshiping God, they did not really mean it.

This brings to our minds something that the Bible is very faithful to us about. God looks on the heart. The outward activity is important, but the worshiper must mean it. The human heart is such that religious people can get into the habit of doing things and not mean them. They can go through the routines that they have learned or that are desirable, but they do not really mean the very thing they are doing. They are not sincere. But God is not mocked. God looks on the heart.

The prophets knew this, and they preached to the people of their time, warning them about an insincere approach to God, warning them that God would not tolerate it. While God is very gracious to a humble and contrite heart, the Bible reveals that God resists the proud. It does not make any difference to God who a man is, or where he is. If a person is proud in his heart before God, then God will have nothing to do with him. God gives grace to the humble. But the human heart tends toward pride. People find it easy to be proud.

It was the business of the prophets to remind the people of these things and to call upon them to change their ways. The prophets had a word for that. It is the great word of all Old Testament ministers. The prophets laid down one first call that came to the heart of every one of God's people: "Repent."

"Repent" means to pass judgment on ourselves, to examine ourselves whether we are in the faith. We should watch our own hearts. We can fool ourselves so easily and deceive ourselves to such disastrous results. The prophets held up a mirror in front of God's people showing them the real meaning of the Word of God and the law of God. They urged God's people to judge themselves so that they should not be judged. This was the kind of ministry that Amos presented in his day and time, using impressive procedures.

> The words of Amos, who was among the herdmen of Tekoa, which he saw concerning Israel in the days of Uzziah king of Judah, and in the days of Jeroboam the son of Joash king of Israel, two years before the earthquake. And he said, The Lord will roar from Zion (Amos 1:1-2).

This language was his opening text. The "roaring" refers to the sound of a lion. The implication is clearly that the Lord would come to judge. The Lord would cry out judgment against His people.

> And he said, The Lord will roar from Zion, and utter his voice from Jerusalem; and the habitations of the shepherds shall mourn, and the top of Carmel shall wither (Amos 1:2).

God was going to come and deal with people.

> Thus saith the Lord; For three transgressions of Damascus, and for four, I will not turn away the punishment thereof (Amos 1:3).

Amos told the people why. Damascus was far away, up in the north in the country of Syria.

> Thus saith the Lord; For three transgressions of Gaza, and for four, I will not turn away the punishment thereof (Amos 1:6).

Gaza was in the land of the Philistines, down in the south. These were cities outside of Judah and Israel. Amos was pointing out God was going to judge the sins of Damascus and the transgressions of Gaza.

> Thus saith the Lord; For three transgressions of Tyrus, and for four, I will not turn away the punishment thereof (Amos 1:9).

North of Israel and a little to the west, in the land of Phoenicia by the Mediterranean sea, was the city of Tyre, also a foreign

city. Amos said God was certainly going to judge the city of
Tyre.

> Thus saith the Lord; For three transgressions of Edom, and for
> four, I will not turn away the punishment thereof (Amos 1:11).

Then Amos turned to the east, across the Jordan and over into
the desert, among those people who were related but did not
belong to Israel. He pointed out that for their sin God would
certainly judge them. Close to Edom was the country of the
Ammonites, who also were related to the Israelites although
they were not a part of them. The Ammonites had sinned, and
God would certainly judge them.

> Thus saith the Lord; For three transgressions of Moab, and for
> four, I will not turn away the punishment thereof; because he
> burned the bones of the king of Edom into lime: but I will send
> a fire upon Moab, and it shall devour the palaces of Kirioth . . .
> (Amos 2:1-2).

Amos pointed out how God would judge them. Note that
Amos mentioned all these cities on the outskirts, on the
fringes of Judah and Israel: Damascus to the north, an Assyrian city; Gaza to the south, a Philistine city; Tyrus to the
northwest, a Phoenician city; Edom to the east, in the desert;
Ammon to the east; and Moab to the east.

> Thus saith the Lord; For three transgressions of Judah, and for
> four, I will not turn away the punishment thereof (Amos 2:4).

Amos was preaching in Israel, the northern kingdom. From
there he pointed over to the southern kingdom and said God
would certainly judge them. The procedure of Amos is effective. As long as Amos was pointing at people somewhere else,
noting their sins and saying that God would not condone them
but judge them, he could get the consent of his hearers that it
should really be so.

Amos was preaching in a time when Israel was divided into
north and south. In the north were the ten tribes of Israel; in
the south were the two tribes of Judah. The north was large
and rich; the south was small and poor. But the south was
closer to God. The south was more orthodox, because it included Jerusalem; the north did not have the city of God. The
south had Solomon's temple; the north did not. In Israel was a
large prosperous, ungodly, and immoral group of people; in

Judah was a smaller, poorer, more spiritually minded and more orthodox people. And between these two there was a great deal of bitterness from time to time. They often had war between them.

David in an earlier generation came from the south, the southern kingdom called Judah. The northern kingdom was called Israel, or "Samaria," after its capital city. Because half the tribe of Manasseh lived in the south, the name "Manasseh" was sometimes used for the southern kingdom, and the name "Ephraim," the other son of Joseph, for the northern kingdom. But always it was true that the north was large and populous, while the south was small and relatively poor. But the south was more staunch and stern. The north had fine agricultural country—broad, fertile plains. The south was a mountainous country with poor people. But the southerners were a very sturdy lot.

That was the general situation. The feeling between the two was just about what could be expected. They were not happy in each other's presence, and they certainly did not get along with each other. Amos in this particular situation was called to a rather awkward circumstance: born in the south, he was called to preach in the north. The north was wealthy; the people had money. But Amos was a country man, a farmer's son, a keeper of sycamore trees, and also a herdsman at the time when he was called to preach.

And so a farmer was called to go into a sophisticated section of the country where people lived mostly in the cities and towns and where they would have the urban frame of mind. This country preacher came there to tell them to get right with God. It was obvious that Amos would not be popular. But we should notice how wise Amos was. Amos began his message by pointing at people who lived at a distance. Having established his principle of judgment by God, he then narrowed his focus and spoke directly to those living in Israel.

> Thus saith the Lord; For three transgressions of Israel, and for
> four, I will not turn away the punishment thereof; because they
> sold the righteous for silver, and the poor for a pair of shoes
> (Amos 2:6).

We should notice how the kinds of sin varied in each case. With the pagan people—with Damascus, Gaza, Tyrus,

Edom, Ammon, and Moab—the sin was cruelty. It was un-
kindness, viciousness, and atrocities which they committed
against each other. God holds man to account for man's inhumanity to man. Those pagan nations did not have the light
that the people of Judah had or even the light that the people
of Israel had. But the light of their own conscience and the
light of nature would be enough for them to know that when
they were thus harming God's creatures and their fellowmen,
they were actually sinning against God.

Now when it came to Judah, Amos did not accuse the
people of cruelty. We do not know whether Judah was cruel.
It is conceivable that they were not. This was not the accusa-
tion against them.

> Thus saith the Lord; For three transgressions of Judah, and for
> four, I will not turn away the punishment thereof; because they
> have despised the law of the Lord, and have not kept his com-
> mandments, and their lies caused them to err, after the which
> their fathers have walked (Amos 2:4).

Judah was held responsible because, having received the
Word of God, they did not follow it. That was just as sinful in
the sight of God as the Ammonites' ripping up pregnant
women in time of war. God saw those things, and He said He
would judge them. But Judah was to be judged in the same
tone of voice because, having the Word of God, they did not
keep it.

What did Amos say in the case of Israel? These people did
not have the worship of God in the temple. They did not have
the city of Jerusalem, and they did not have the levitical
priesthood. And so they were not as well-trained and taught
in the Word of God as Judah. But they knew enough not to do
unkind things and unjust deeds to their brothers.

Amos noted three characteristics of the sin of Israel. First,
they were unjust. They exploited the poor; second, they were
immoral. In verse 7 Amos pointed out that they "turn aside
the way of the meek: and a man and his father will go in unto
the same maid." In verse 8 he noted their irreverence: "They
lay themselves down upon clothes laid to pledge by every
altar, and they drink the wine of the condemned in the house
of their god." Thus they were unjust, immoral, irreverent.
These are not so much human cruelties. It is not so much that

the people of Israel were doing things that were of a violent nature physically. But there was an unfairness, an injustice in dealing with people. There was immorality in their personal conduct. There was irreverence toward God. All these, as Amos noted, were systems of sin that prevailed in Israel.

Amos then pointed out how their history showed God's gracious acts. "Yet destroyed I the Amorite before them" (Amos 2:9). Amos reminded them that God brought them into blessings.

> Also I brought you up from the land of Egypt, and led you forty years through the wilderness, to possess the land of the Amorite. And I raised up of your sons for prophets, and of your young men for Nazarites. Is it not even thus, O ye children of Israel? saith the Lord (Amos 2:10-11).

The prophet reminded them that God demonstrably blessed them in the past, and He deserved something better than that they should neglect Him and turn away from Him now.

> But ye gave the Nazarites wine to drink (Amos 2:12).

The Nazarites were a class of people who in serving God made it a particular point not to drink wine. They lived a very careful and rather ascetic life, in which they devoted themselves totally and entirely to doing the will of God. The kind of people who will not do some things—because of their faith they will not participate in certain "worldly amusements"— are sometimes an annoyance to other believers. They make other people feel uncomfortable. And so it was with Israel. The people gave the Nazarites wine to drink. Thus they tried to break down that style of careful living which the Nazarites practiced; they tried to get the Nazarites to act just as worldly as they themselves. God noticed that kind of treatment, and He would not overlook it.

> But ye gave the Nazarites wine to drink; and commanded the prophets, saying, Prophesy not (Amos 2:12).

God sent the prophets to the people to warn them, to remind them, to show them the will of God. But the people of Israel asked these preachers to "pipe down." God noticed that, too. In all of this that we have been studying here in Amos, we have seen how God looks at the heart of people and sees their sin.

In chapter 3 Amos continues to deal with these people. The Book of Amos was probably not prepared as one message. It was not just one sermon. This may have been what we call a notebook. Sometimes three or four verses have one idea, the next two or three verses will have a different idea, and then somewhere else it will be something else, so that the book seems almost disjointed. As we go through the verses we can sense the general message that the man Amos was giving.

So far in our study of this book we have recognized the fact that Amos was pointing out sin. Amos was warning the people that God would surely judge their sin.

> Surely the Lord God will do nothing, but he revealeth his secret unto his servants the prophets (Amos 3:7).

This is perhaps an awkward way of saying, "Surely the Lord God will not do anything with His people that He does not reveal to His servants, His prophets."

> The lion hath roared, who will not fear? the Lord God hath spoken, who can but prophesy? (Amos 3:8).

It seems to me that Amos was saying, "You will just have to let me say what is in my heart." God has spoken and the lion has roared, so who will not be afraid? We just cannot help but be impressed by it. "The Lord God hath spoken, who can but prophesy?" Then Amos moved on to preach about these things.

In chapter 4 there is a new aspect of the message of Amos. "Hear this word, ye kine of Bashan." Here again we have to pause with a word like "kine." Ordinarily we do not use it, but it is simply an old English word meaning "cattle."

"You cattle of Bashan." Why would Amos call the people cattle? We may remember that when Israel made their idols, they made a golden calf. When Jeroboam set up altars to worship in Israel, the northern kingdom, he made calves as idols. Jeroboam had spent time in exile in Egypt in the days of Solomon. He returned at the request of the northern kingdom and led the people in breaking away from the southern kingdom, from Rehoboam, the son of Solomon. They established the northern kingdom as a separate kingdom, with Jeroboam as their leader. Jeroboam was a man who had a great deal of Egyptian experience. When he set up altars in the northern kingdom, to replace worshiping in Jerusalem, he made images of calves that would remind us of the worship of the Egyptians. Also the nearby Assyrians worshiped cattle and oxen. The words of Amos are a sarcastic reference to these people who were having pagan tendencies.

> The Lord God hath sworn by his holiness, that, lo, the days shall come upon you, that he will take you away with hooks, and your posterity with fishhooks (Amos 4:2).

Bethel and Gilgal were two places of worship. "Come to Bethel, and transgress; at Gilgal multiply transgression" (Amos 4:4). What Amos said to these people in a challenging, provocative way was, "Come to your church services and sin. Come to Bethel, your place of worship, and transgress. At Gilgal, your place of worship, where you come to worship God, multiply transgressions." He pointed out that their way of worshiping God was unsound.

> . . . Bring your sacrifices every morning, and your tithes after three years: and offer a sacrifice of thanksgiving with leaven (Amos 4:4-5).

The use in Scripture of the phrase "with leaven" implies "uncleanness." Sacrifice was to be made of unleavened bread—bread without yeast in it. When there was any yeast or "leaven" in the bread, it was not considered proper for sacrificial purposes. What this Scripture means to me as a preacher is "Go ahead and preach your sermon, full of your own human conceit as you are preaching." Such preaching would be "with leaven." Amos was saying in effect, "Come to your church services at Bethel and Gilgal and multiply transgressions, offering up your sacrifices insincerely to God. You go through the motions of worship but you do not mean it." That is the way Amos put it.

> And I also have given you cleanness of teeth in all your cities, and want of bread in all your places: yet have ye not returned unto me, saith the Lord (Amos 4:6).

This is a poetic way of saying "I sent famine, yet you have not come back to me." Amos reminded the people that God let them have the calamity of famine, but they did not turn to God.

> And also I have withholden the rain from you. . . . So two or
> three cities wandered unto one city, to drink water . . . yet
> have ye not returned unto me, saith the Lord (Amos 4:7-8).

God sent drought. Those people understood that when God
did not send them rain, when God in any way interfered with
the crop processes, God was judging them. God had dealt
thus with them. He let them have drought. It did not rain.
"Yet have ye not returned unto me, saith the Lord."

> I have smitten you with blasting and mildew: when your gar-
> dens and your vineyards and your fig trees and your olive trees
> increased, the palmerworm devoured them: yet have ye not
> returned unto me, saith the Lord (Amos 4:9).

The people had diseased crops. When the gardens and the
vineyards and fruit trees increased, the palmerworm de-
voured them. We will remember the message of Joel, that
whenever there were pests destroying the crops, it was evidence of the judgment of God.

> I have sent among you the pestilence after the manner of
> Egypt: your young men have I slain with the sword . . . yet
> have ye not returned unto me, saith the Lord (Amos 4:10).

In other words, Amos said, "I sent you trouble. I actually sent
you war."

> I have overthrown some of you, as God overthrew Sodom and
> Gomorrah . . . yet have ye not returned unto me, saith the
> Lord (Amos 4:11).

"I sent you natural calamities like an earthquake or a tornado
or a fire, yet you have not returned to me, says the Lord."
Here is an amazing thing, and we recall the Book of Joel in
speaking about this: God in mercy, trying to wake up His
people, lets them have trouble. So He sends them famine:
that is trouble. Drought, no rain: that is trouble. Crop diseases: that is trouble. Pests that destroy the crops: that is real
trouble. Sickness and epidemics, diseases, pestilence: that
was trouble. War, with many casualties: that was trouble. And
then great natural calamities, like earthquakes and volcanic
eruptions: that was trouble. And in all this they did not turn to
God. They were incorrigible.

> Therefore thus will I do unto thee, O Israel: and because I will
> do this unto thee, prepare to meet thy God, O Israel (Amos
> 4:12).

The prophet was not preaching about pagan people. He was not writing about people who do not know God. This is the way God deals with His own people. It is enough to make believers humble and to cry to God in themselves; and to ask God to be merciful to keep them from ever having to be dealt with this way. God is too faithful to His own people to let them go on in foolishness indefinitely. He keeps His hand over them. He calls them. He wants them to judge themselves. They should humble themselves before Him, cast themselves upon His mercy and let Him work in them. But in the event that in their foolishness and in their conceit they blandly go their own way, they will be brought about sharply to face God.

We should not understand that this whole statement should be applied only to weak people. It was not the weak who are being warned; it is the callous and indifferent. It is not those who blunder into things that are wrong, but it is those who carelessly go on practicing what is wrong.

Because the people would not take note of what was happening, they never called upon themselves to review before God. So Amos warned them: "Prepare to meet thy God, O Israel."

In chapter 5 Amos presents the positive side of his message, and indeed it is the real heart of the message.

> For thus saith the Lord unto the house of Israel, Seek ye me,
> and ye shall live (Amos 5:4).

No matter where sinners are and no matter what they have done, no matter how much they have failed, he says, "Seek ye me, and ye shall live."

> But seek not Bethel, nor enter into Gilgal, and pass not to
> Beersheba: for Gilgal shall surely go into captivity, and Bethel
> shall come to nought. Seek the Lord, and ye shall live (Amos
> 5:5-6).

If this declaration were being applied to our times it would be as much as to say, "Don't be satisfied with stopping with a denomination. Don't just get into a denomination. Get into the Lord. Come to the Lord." It is not enough to be a member of a church; the believer needs to be a member of the Lord Jesus Christ. Churches are good to help a believer to get to know God. But if the believer does not get to know God in a church, it can be a snare to him. A person could join a church and then think everything is all right. But no matter what church he belonged to, if he did not belong to the Lord Jesus Christ, nothing would help. That seems to be Amos's message here. "Seek not Bethel, nor enter into Gilgal. . . . Seek the Lord, and ye shall live."

Certainly believers could attend church, but they should complete the sentence: they should come to church to worship God. Worshipers should make it a point when they come to church to come into the presence of God. They should go to prayer meeting to pray to God. True religion is what God is looking for. "Seek the Lord, and ye shall live."

Amos then began to promise several things.

> Seek good, and not evil, that ye may live: and so the Lord, the God of hosts, shall be with you, as ye have spoken. Hate the evil, and love the good, and establish judgment in the gate: it may be that the Lord God of hosts will be gracious unto the remnant of Joseph (Amos 5:14-15).

This is the great call of Amos.

> Woe unto you that desire the day of the Lord! (Amos 5:18).

The day of the Lord, according to the prophets, was the time when God would begin to work in a special way with people. There are some who, when they look out upon world affairs, even the affairs of a community, will say, "If only God would work! What we need is for the Lord to do something." Amos would say: "Do you really mean that? Do you know what would really happen if the Lord started to work in the community? 'Woe unto you that desire the day of the Lord! to what end is it for you? the day of the Lord is darkness, and not light'" (Amos 5:18). He said God would bring judgment and not mercy.

Today in the church, believers need to remember this when they turn to call upon God. Until their sins have been dealt with, there can be no happiness, no satisfaction. Surely believers should turn and call on the Lord. They should seek the Lord that they might live. But it must be a case of seeking the Lord by confessing their sins. They cannot come into the presence of God as they are. They must come to God as He is and acknowledge their transgressions before Him.

Amos warned his people it would be "As if a man did flee from a lion, and a bear met him." There are some who have trouble, because some things in this world are not satisfactory. They have been getting along with their life, but things have not been going well. Life has not been satisfactory, and so they may say what is needed is that God should do something. Sometimes in their agony such persons may pray, "O Lord, do something! Come right in here and do something!" What they sometimes do not realize is that when they are asking the Lord to come right in and do something, He might just start in with them. Their lifestyle could be a good place to start doing something. It could mean making changes at the very outset, and then other matters could be fixed up.

Amos wrote that it could be "as if a man did flee from a lion" because circumstances were bothering him. But when he cried out, "Lord, Lord," Amos said it was as if he met a bear, because when this person met the Lord, the Lord would deal in judgment. Amos went on to point out: "Or went into the house, and leaned his hand on the wall, and a serpent bit him" (Amos 5:19). This implies that, although a man should need support of some kind and lean against a wall with that comfortable feeling, "Well, the Lord will take care of me," in the very place where he put his hand, a serpent would come out and bite him. Judgment can be painful.

Amos was very much concerned about the complacency of his people. They seemed to think, "Oh well, if we get into trouble we will just call on the Lord." But it is not quite that simple. It can be done simply, but it has much more profound meaning than that. Turning to the Lord always requires that the person be willing to yield himself into God's hands and let Him have His way in the heart.

> Shall not the day of the Lord be darkness, and not light? even
> very dark, and no brightness in it? (Amos 5:20).

For people who have been wayward, worldly, callous, and indifferent to cry to God to come and bless them, they should expect that the first thing God would do would be to judge them.

> I hate, I despise your feast days, and I will not smell in your solemn assemblies. Though ye offer me burnt offerings and your meat offerings, I will not accept them: neither will I regard the peace offerings of your fat beasts. Take thou away from me the noise of thy songs; for I will not hear the melody of thy viols. But let judgment run down as waters, and righteousness as a mighty stream (Amos 5:21-24).

This language in its stately old English phrases is impressive to us, but it does not get quite as close to us as the Hebrew tongue got to Israel in the days of Amos. What Amos means is that God was saying to the people, "I hate and despise your feast days." Those feast days were special services, when the worshiper came for special celebration in the sight of God. Amos reports God as saying, "I will not smell in your solemn assemblies." Amos here refers to God's appreciating the sacrifices of "sweet smelling savor," the perfumed sacrifices. Perfume always had to do with thanksgiving and singing praise to God. When God said, "I will not smell in your solemn assemblies," He meant that when they came to praise God in their prayer meetings, He would not listen to them. So God was saying, "I am sick and tired of your special services. When you have your special prayer meetings, I will not even listen to you."

Amos goes on. "Though ye offer me burnt offerings and your meat offerings, I will not accept them." I can understand what this means when I remember that my burnt offering is Jesus Christ. And my peace offering is Jesus Christ. When I come into the presence of God, I bring the Lord Jesus Christ. When I come into the presence of God I come singing, "At the cross, at the cross where I first saw the light, and the burden of my heart rolled away." It is for me in the presence of God to say, "The old rugged cross, so despised by the world, has a wondrous attraction for me." I sing these songs and I say these things as I come into the presence of God, pleading the blood of the Lord Jesus Christ, who is my Sacrifice.

Can we understand what Amos is saying to us? There could be conditions surrounding our coming into the presence of God, so that when we start talking about the sacrifice of the

Lord Jesus Christ, it would make God sick and tired to have us talking about that. What would such conditions be? When we say with our mouths that Christ died for us, but in our hearts we do not serve Him.

"But let judgment run down as waters, and righteousness as a mighty stream" (Amos 5:24). It is for me to be sincere. "A humble and a contrite heart the Lord will not despise." Hypocrites do not even fool all human beings with their superficial activities in church, and they certainly would not fool God. But that is what Israel was trying to do in those days.

We would expect that Amos was not a very popular preacher. But he was a powerful one, I am sure. In chapter 6 he goes right down the line on this very idea.

Woe to them that are at ease in Zion . . . (Amos 6:1).

Amos was not talking about Bethel and Gilgal. He was not talking about those who were wrong in their thinking, or who were promoting unsound religious activities. He was talking about Zion, in the very center of Jerusalem. "Woe to them that are at ease in Zion, and trust in the mountain of Samaria."

Ye that put far away the evil day, and cause the seat of violence
to come near (Amos 6:3).

"Putting far away the evil day" is saying in effect, "Oh, I do not think anything is going to happen to us now. Nothing will happen to us yet. I think things are going to go pretty good. I believe it will be better than it has been." Someone might say, "But unless we seek the Lord and unless we get right with God, unless we repent in our doings, then God will not have dealings with us," and the answer could be, "Oh, we will be all right. It will not happen yet. Someday God may judge, but not now."

Such "put far away the evil day, and cause the seat of violence to come near," people thus ignore and disregard the day of judgment in that way, they actually cause God to bring judgment sooner.

The phrase "that lie upon beds of ivory, and stretch themselves upon their couches" describes how the people took their ease. They just lay down as it were and enjoyed themselves and rested in all the blessings they had. "And eat the lambs out of the flock, and the calves out of the midst of the stall." Everything seemed to be happy and satisfying.

That chant to the sound of the viol, and invent to themselves
instruments of music, like David (Amos 6:5).

David was a great man to praise and worship God. He used
certain musical instruments. So the people of Israel had
plenty of money and bought themselves musical instruments
like David. They had choirs and orchestras that performed
great music and sang great anthems. Their music was the
great music of the church. Have we ever wondered about that
in our day? Have we ever wondered how often some of our
greatest musical compositions are put on almost like a show?
Do we realize that in many cases these anthems and pieces
were composed by men who were trying to honor God? This
is so obvious when we hear Handel's *Messiah* being sung. The
composer intended to honor God when he used those great
verses of Scripture and put them to music in the way he did.
He sincerely meant those words when he wrote that music.
We need to take these things to heart and let Amos speak to
us, because Amos would warn us about our tendency to in-
dulge ourselves when we make for ourselves instruments like
David and then do as Isaiah did.

In chapter 7 Amos writes that the Lord God showed him
several things. God showed him grasshoppers eating everything, and that was a picture of what would happen to Israel.
Amos called out to God and said, "Oh, don't do that! Israel
can't stand that, being consumed that way!" Then God
showed him fire, because God would judge with fire. Again
Amos cried out, "O Lord God, cease, I beseech thee: by
whom shall Jacob arise? for he is small." Then God showed
him a man standing in the midst of Israel with a plumbline, a
carpenter's instrument for judging what is straight up and
down. This was a way of revealing that God would deal with
His people by bringing a demand for sincerity and righteousness; every man would have to be right before God.

We conclude our look at Amos by reminding ourselves that
the one thing God wants from every one of us is that we
should in honesty and sincerity look into His face, see Him as
He is, and let the truth judge us as we are. At the end of his
book Amos wrote a wonderful word of promise: God will
greatly bless those who put their trust in Him.

OBADIAH

† † †

OBADIAH DID NOT preach to Israel. He is like both Nahum and Jonah in that respect. Obadiah preached to Edom.

The original name for Edom was Esau. Rebecca, the wife of Isaac, gave birth to twin sons. The older was Esau; the younger was Jacob. As it turned out, each got another name: Esau's name became Edom, meaning practically the same thing; but Jacob's name was changed to Israel, which meant something far different.

"Esau" refers to the flesh, and "Edom" to humanity. In the Hebrew language the word *Edom* and the word *Adam* are very closely related. The Adam of Genesis and the Edom of Isaac's family are, as far as their names are concerned, very closely related.

The name "Jacob" refers to a certain conniving ambitious spirit that the second twin had in him. The name "Israel" refers to a dignity and a nobility that the man attained because of his persistence with God. A change came over Jacob. But no such transformation occurred in the case of Esau; thus "Esau" and "Edom" meant virtually the same thing. On the other hand, as "Esau" and "Edom" refer to "the flesh," so the two names "Jacob" and "Israel" refer to "the spirit."

When we think about spirit we are thinking in the perspective that leads the mind to heaven. The heart is turned to the invisible things of God and related to God. "God is a Spirit: and they that worship him must worship him in spirit and in truth" (John 4:24). The word "spirit" implies something of conscious relationship with God. The Spirit of God is a Person; but when we speak of being related to God in spirit, we mean as the Holy Spirit deals with our spirit, a matter of our consciousness and our will and our commitment to God.

The word "flesh" means far more than a person's physical body. It means everything about a person as a human being, everything that the word "human" implies. It includes everything of self, since everything about self belongs to the flesh. Everything about vanity, everything about pride, everything about appetite, everything about imagination, everything that has to do with the things that appeal to me personally belongs to the flesh. All that has to do with my "ego" belongs to the flesh. But all that has to do with my soul, with my eternal relationship with God in Christ, refers to the spirit. We need to recognize these two elements because in the New Testament it is revealed that believers in Christ have both principles in them.

The children of Israel are the people who followed in the faith of the man Israel, who had an abiding and persistent faith in God, and who clung to God for His blessing. "I will not let thee go except thou bless me" is the truth that made Israel, and this belongs in the spirit. Esau in the flesh was a person who wanted things for himself—things that he could understand and things he possessed. When Obadiah preached to Edom, he was preaching to people who actually were related to the Jews, that is, to Israel. Jacob and Esau were brothers, and so their descendants were in a sense cousins. This fact helps us to understand the Book of Obadiah.

While it is true that Obadiah's message was given to the nation of Edom historically, I feel that the focus of this book is the message of the Word of God to "the flesh." The flesh is closely related to believers in Christ. In our own families, communities, and cities, there are people who do not belong to God, but who have heard the Gospel. They do know what the church stands for. There is a word to be spoken to these people. They are people related to the church. In a sense they are the human and physical "in-laws" of the church. They know about the church. They live in the area around where the Gospel is known. They could be called strangers, since humanly speaking they are not strangers. But spiritually speaking they have no relationship with God.

I believe the message of Obadiah to Edom is very close to the kind of message that should be spoken to people who live in a community where there are Christian churches but do nothing about it. These are people who live in a community where many children go to Sunday school, yet never take their own children there. They are people who have brothers and sisters, uncles and aunts and cousins who belong to the church, but in heart despise them for it. Such people are to my mind in the spiritual category and class of these people of Edom. Obadiah was the messenger, and he had a message for them. The message to Edom is a message to all flesh.

In this short Book of Obadiah we find two outstanding characteristics of the flesh. The first is pride.

> The pride of thine heart hath deceived thee, thou that dwellest in the clefts of the rock, whose habitation is high; that saith in his heart, Who shall bring me down to the ground? Though thou exalt thyself as the eagle, and though thou set thy nest among the stars, thence will I bring thee down, saith the Lord (Obadiah 1:3-4).

No doubt many believers know perhaps only far too well, and with sadness in their hearts, the number of times that others have proudly despised their "religion." When that attitude is examined it will be found that it is inspired by plain, old-fashioned, unvarnished pride. I mean pride in the sight of God. Obadiah would tell such that their pride is an offense to God, and that almighty God has given His word that He will strip that pride from them. He will destroy every one of them.

The sinfulness of pride abounds as long as men live and wherever they live. It is everywhere, all the time. Pride can keep a person from praying. Pride can keep him from carrying a Bible. And yet the human heart is so tricky a person could be fooled about that. Obadiah would stand there, and put his finger on the first fault of flesh: pride. A person can be high and lifted up in his own esteem, but almighty God said,

"Though thou set thy nest among the stars, thence will I bring thee down." That was the first word that was spoken to Edom. The second word is in the tenth verse.

> For thy violence against thy brother Jacob shame shall cover thee, and thou shalt be cut off for ever (Obadiah 1:10).

I wonder if any of us realize how dangerous it is to sneer at a humble, sincere Christian. We should never ridicule a believer. We should be careful not to be unkind to anyone who names the name of the Lord Jesus Christ. There are some believers in Christ who will not be wise after our ideas of wisdom; but if they are earnest and sincere, the Lord looks on the heart. Some of these people in their piety may seem closer to the Lord than others, but become overweening in their manner. Our attitude and our spirit toward them should not be one of pride or violence. Man's inhumanity to man is a scandal on the face of the earth, but it is a serious thing with God. God simply will not approve a strong man stepping on a weak one. Persons who understand the Scriptures have a responsibility to be kind to others who do not understand the Scriptures. Abraham would not walk with Lot, but Abraham prayed for Lot. Abraham would not live with Lot, but when Lot got into trouble Abraham organized a rescue party to go and deliver him. The disposition of being interested in the welfare of others belongs to those who believe the Gospel.

Obadiah details the cruel manner in which Esau (Edom) took advantage of Jacob (Israel) in the time of his calamity.

> In the day that thou stoodest on the other side, in the day that the strangers carried away captive his forces, and foreigners entered into his gates, and cast lots upon Jerusalem, even thou wast as one of them. But thou shouldest not have looked on the day of thy brother in the day that he became a stranger; neither shouldest thou have rejoiced over the children of Judah in the day of their destruction; neither shouldest thou have spoken proudly in the day of distress. Thou shouldest not have entered into the gate of my people in the day of their calamity; yea, thou shouldest not have looked on their affliction in the day of their calamity, nor have laid hands on their substance in the day of their calamity; neither shouldest thou have stood in the crossway, to cut off those of his that did escape; neither shouldest thou have delivered up those of his that did remain in the day of distress (Obadiah 1:11-14).

In the rest of his book Obadiah describes the destruction which would come upon Edom in the will of God. In the Scripture there is so much emphasis upon the grace of God with so much description of His loving compassion that it is actually startling to read that He will destroy those who persist in wickedness. The Book of Obadiah is a clear revelation of the judgment of God on the wicked.

JONAH

† † †

DO YOU REALIZE that God gives each person his own task to perform? The providence of God is involved in the day-by-day experience of the believer. Would this be true even of the unbeliever? The Bible talks primarily to people who believe in God. It is after people have turned to Him that God talks to them. Yet I am disposed to think that God intervenes in the life of everyone. Such verses as "Thou God seest me" express truth for all. "He knoweth the way I take." Yes, He does!

The strongest argument that I can offer for this conviction is the passage that tells me that God sees each sparrow falling to the ground. If He sees a sparrow falling to the ground, I suspect He sees each human being. When He says the hairs of our heads are numbered, that is enough to quiet our souls. God knows all things, and He holds all things in His hand. And He has His will about each person. God lets the situation develop in which a believer can serve Him.

This can be seen in the Book of Jonah. Jonah is the name of the book because the book is the story of a man called Jonah. We often call him a prophet, and it seems he was. Jonah was a preacher, although there is nothing to indicate that he was a priest. We might call him a lay preacher. He was not a preacher as we understand the role today, as there were no congregations then as now, nor was he one of the tribe of the Levites.

The story of Jonah is the story of a man who was given a task to perform. It is a simple story, widely known. Because of its unusual features, it is often distorted. At times people stress one aspect without getting the story as a whole.

The story comes to us as a narrative, straightforward and clear. We know that Jonah preached in Nineveh, but not a single sermon of his is listed. We do not know how much time he spent there, although it was possibly forty days. We know that he was there, that he preached and had a powerful effect upon the Ninevites. We are told the story without extensive detail.

The reader is not told what kind of a man Jonah was, nor how he performed his task. Jonah's assignment was not given to a whole class of people; rather, it was specific: "Jonah, you do this." It was one man, under God, facing his life. He had a task to do. "Go to Nineveh (which was a great city), and tell them what God is going to do." The point is, Jonah was given a task. We might assume the people would not want to hear the message. It was not a pleasant word Jonah was to take. It was a warning of judgment and destruction.

The Christian in his daily living may face a situation that would raise the objection of other people if he were to do the right thing. Just imagine someone standing up in your city and openly taking the best opportunity he had to say that the people in the city are wrong—not just a special group, but all of us. Or take the example of a woman in her home. How many times a woman has to turn to God quietly in her heart and trust in Him. The things that she can see about her are wrong. However, if she were to speak out about it, she would offend. She has to live with her people. It entails a great sense of responsibility. Or take a young person who wants to be a Christian. What a difficult thing for her to witness! I remember so well a girl in Alabama writing to me. She was at that time about fourteen or fifteen years old, and I remember one sentence in her letter that stuck in my heart: "It's so hard to be a Christian in high school!" But she *was* a Christian and we were glad to think we had some share in helping her with her witness and testimony. This is the way it is with many of us.

It is difficult to bring a message to people urging them to change their ways. Yet any witness for Christ faces this, and the believer can expect opposition. This is the way it was with Jonah. God said, "You do this," and Jonah went the other way. This is not too surprising. The road Jonah was asked to travel was hard, so he went the other way. Details are few. We know that Jonah boarded a ship going in another direction. Jonah did not do as he was told. He disobeyed God. Perhaps many people today could sympathize with Jonah and say, "He did not want to be involved, so he went the other way."

The next thing we notice is that God blocked the course of Jonah's disobedience. The book does not tell us what awaited Jonah in Tarshish, nor what God was thinking when He sent the storm. God prepared a storm that threatened the ship on which Jonah sailed. The sailors were mortally afraid and sought to discover who was at fault to cause this judgment from almighty God. Jonah himself came forward and told them, "I am the man." Then they had in mind, "What in the world are we going to do with you?" He said, "There is only one thing to do. Get rid of me. Throw me overboard."

The storm was no punishment. God did not send that storm to punish Jonah or the sailors. This was His way of getting a man turned around who was going in the wrong direction. Jonah admitted his responsibility and yielded to this new situation. He told the sailors what to do. His instruction was simple: "Take me up, and cast me into the sea." It was not easy for these sailors to do that. They came and asked Jonah to forgive them. They even asked almighty God to forgive them.

Now comes the part that fascinates people so much and causes many to stumble. God arranged for Jonah to be swallowed by a great fish. All God had to do was to prepare the fish and have him there on time. When I say "all," I remember that only God could prepare such a fish. This implies that God knew years before that Jonah was going to do just as he did, and He had the whale there at the right time so that the whale swallowed Jonah.

God is infinite—infinitely great. He knows all about everyone. This is of great comfort to Christians as they live their lives. There will be no sudden surprise to catch God off guard. If we are turning to Him to pray, He knows what we have need of before we ask it.

We find that Jonah was swallowed by the whale, and even more amazing, he was still alive. A great many people have trouble about that. This is not necessary. Simply take God's Word as it is! This man Jonah was conscious there in the belly of the whale and then, in that extremity, he prayed to God. A believer can understand that. When a person gets down to the very bottom, and everything is falling in on top of him, a person will pray as he has never prayed before. This was Jonah's experience.

There is no prolonged reasoning on the part of Jonah. We might think of this: to be sure, he had disobeyed God. Don't you think Jonah knew that? Certainly Jonah knew he had been disobedient, and don't you think that Jonah knew he was in this plight because of what he had done? Of course! But Jonah believed in God nonetheless.

This reminds us of the Prodigal Son. Remember that the Prodigal left home and spent everything he had. He finally got down to where he was tending swine. As he tried to feed himself with the food that he was giving to the pigs, the truth suddenly struck him. "He came to himself" Scripture puts it. "In my Father's house there is plenty. The servants have enough to eat in my Father's house." When we read the story of the Prodigal in Luke 15, we notice that it never entered the Prodigal's heart and mind to doubt that his father would listen to him. He knew he was unworthy. But he never questioned that his father would hear him. He was right.

Jonah had in mind the God he worshiped and believed in, and the prophet cried out to God for help. In that moment Jonah realized his complete dependence upon God. What he needed now was help. And he found it. Salvation is of the Lord. God can hear—and He does. Jonah was ready to thank God for deliverance and to praise God for His goodness, and so Jonah was put on the dry land.

A person would almost think that this is the end of the story. But this is just part one. Now we come to part two. Jonah was given another chance to do the very thing he had not done: nothing added, nothing taken away. Nineveh was still there, and Nineveh needed the message. God had chosen

Jonah, and now Jonah is ready to follow the Lord's command. Jonah was different now, a chastened servant, and he did as he was told.

There is no description of his manner of preaching. There is no description of his frame of mind. But I am impressed by the fact that when Jonah preached, those people listened and "repented in sackcloth and ashes." They turned to God. No doubt Jonah's preaching had an extra dimension after that whale experience. This would be true for any of us who preach or teach or witness to other people about the Lord; if we have ever been through any truly close experience with God, we have a deeper understanding about all these things.

You may have noticed that sometimes I refer to "the great fish" and again to "the whale." In the Book of Jonah the creature is called a great fish, and in the Gospel of Matthew it is called a whale. Although the Book of Jonah talks about the great fish, the Lord Jesus in speaking about it said, "When he was in the whale's belly. . . ." You know, a great fish is a whale, and a whale is a great fish.

Now when Jonah had so preached and these people had so believed, Nineveh repented—which was a wonderful thing. Then God changed His plans. So far as Jonah was concerned, it looked as if God changed His mind. The message that Jonah gave was from God. It was not that Jonah was such a smart man, or clever, but that he was a faithful man. He preached God's message, and it was effectual. Jonah had been disobedient, but his disobedience did not hinder his usefulness.

In your experience have there been times when you did things which you should not have done? Do you think that is going to hinder you in the future? Not at all. I know that some foolish thing I may have done may put me at a disadvantage. I may have spent my money foolishly and now I do not have any money. But I can turn to God, "forgetting the things that are behind." This is what Jonah did. He went to Nineveh and preached. God blessed his preaching and Nineveh repented.

Jonah was upset. Jonah was disturbed because God changed His plan and spared Nineveh. Jonah understood what God had told him He would do: in forty days He would destroy Nineveh. Jonah now saw that God did not do it. That shook Jonah. It is strange when we stop to think about it: the man who failed to do as he was told, the man who disobeyed God, was the man who could not stand God's changing His way.

But then a wonderful thing happened. Instead of God rebuking Jonah and exposing him before the whole world as being such a limited person, God arranged a situation in which Jonah could learn. God prepared a gourd that grew up and gave Jonah shade. Then a worm ate into the gourd and caused it to die so that the shade was gone. Jonah was upset about this. God came to him and asked him, "Have you any reason to feel bad because that gourd withered up?"

"Yes, I have," said Jonah. Now the shade was gone. Yes, he had reason to be upset. He was unhappy.

God said, "You are unhappy because with the gourd gone, you are exposed now to the sun and you are hot. Should not I have been unhappy to think about all those people in Nineveh who would have been destroyed? Think of all the children who are there, who do not know their right hand from their left: just youngsters, innocent people. And all the cattle, that are there. Don't you think that I should be conscious of their need?"

The record does not tell what Jonah thought. There is no further record about Jonah. We must remember this book is not primarily about Jonah, nor Nineveh. This book is about God, and how God deals with His people.

When the Word of God is declared, it will affect people. It will lead many to repentance. When people repent, they will be spared because God is not willing that any should perish, but that all should have everlasting life. The purpose of the Book of Jonah is not the history of Jonah, not the character of Jonah, not the history of Nineveh, nor the fate of Nineveh. The purpose of the Book of Jonah is to reveal the truth about our great God, who is merciful and compassionate and not willing that any should perish.

LESSONS FOR JONAH

Jonah is one of the best-known of the Old Testament prophets. But he is known as the disobedient prophet. We may be inclined to think about Jonah in the Old Testament somewhat as we think about Peter in the New Testament, and we will take note of this later. Probably the first thing Jonah needed to learn was that God is sovereign. God is in control. In everyday language we would simply say that He is "Boss." We are reminded of the Scripture that says, "It is not in man to direct his steps." God will accomplish His purpose. His hand is on all things, and He is over all and He will bring His will to pass. The world was created by God, and it is sustained by God. This world is being controlled by God. God is in charge!

It is one of the tragedies of human experience that people find it so easy to think they can do as they please. They go out and act any way they want to and think they should be allowed to get away with it. This is foolish. God is sovereign. He is on the throne, and He is alive and active. We would be wise to remember this.

So this is the first thing Jonah needed to have in mind. He could never get away from God. What God wanted to have done would be done.

The second thing Jonah learned is that God directs His servants. We speak of God's permissive will—what God allows—and His directive will—what God wants. God has a way of overruling and bringing His will to pass whether His servants do or do not want to obey Him. Life as a whole is primarily a matter of obedience. It is surprising how many people have the idea that living depends upon intelligence, reasonableness, and logic. But this is God's world. What I wish or do not wish is unimportant; what counts is what God wants me to do. Contrary to common opinion, a person is not really free to do as he or she pleases. On the surface, it may appear that people are free to go out and make fools of themselves. Yet, there is a limit even to this.

God has a way of overruling. Jonah needed to learn this. He needed to learn that if God wanted him to do something, he would have saved time and trouble if he had done as God wished. This is why we read in the New Testament in the writing of the apostle Paul: "Whatsoever ye do in word or deed, do all in the name of the Lord Jesus, giving thanks to God and the Father by him" (Col. 3:17). Everything that comes before us we should take as from God and we should do it for God's sake—and we will be blessed.

Jonah's disobedience was human; it came naturally. But he needed to learn that disobedience brings distress. A person cannot get away with disobedience without suffering consequences. Providence is under God's control. God is too faithful to let a person get away with such foolishness. In the Scriptures it is written: "Foolishness is bound in the heart of a child; but the rod of correction shall drive it far from him" (Prov. 22:15). If we think of ourselves as children of God, we can understand this: "Foolishness is bound in the heart of a child." Doing things contrary to the will of God is just as natural as the rain falling down to the ground. But "the rod of correction shall drive it far from him." Disobedience brings distress. God has a plan for each one.

Jonah, in distress, learned to pray. He was thrown overboard, and a great fish swallowed him. This was real trouble. In Jonah 2:7 it is recorded: "When my soul fainted within me I remembered the Lord: and my prayer came in unto thee, into thine holy temple." Jonah was not hindered at this time by any feelings of guilt or personal pride. He was in such a state he did not have time to think about anything else. His time was short. He was still alive but seemingly not for long. He cried out to God and learned that God would hear him. In distress, prayer is the way out.

When he was put on the shore, Jonah discovered something else: God's purpose does not change. Before the experience of being thrown into the sea, Jonah had a commission to go to Nineveh and preach. The commission was unchanged. The people in Nineveh could be saved, and God's Word needed to be taken to them. They were going to be told they were wrong: the way they were living was wrong, and God would judge. Jonah was to go and tell them this truth: God will judge you. In judgment, God will destroy. This was the commission, but Jonah had run away from it. Then he became a changed man, and he was again told to do it! He must do the same thing—not added to, not taken from, not revised. God's purpose did not change.

Jonah also learned that God's Word is powerful, regardless of the messenger. In this case the messenger was disobedient Jonah. Jonah walked away from God and went the other way.

But now he was turned around, changed; and when he came to give the message, the Word of God was *un*changed. When it was expressed, it was powerful.

We are reminded of Peter on the day of Pentecost. On that wonderful day when the Holy Spirit came to dwell in the hearts of the believers, they experienced something that became a great demonstration in the city of Jerusalem. Peter got up to preach, to explain, to interpret. Who was Peter? Among other things Peter was a man who denied his Lord, just a matter of weeks before. Peter, changed now by the grace of God, stood up and declared the Word of God with such power that three thousand people were converted and added to the church of the Lord Jesus Christ.

People might say what a marvelous man Peter was! But it was not that Peter was so wonderful. It was a demonstration of how powerful God's Word is. Power belongs to God, regardless of the messenger. Here is a wonderful thing. Although the messenger had been unfaithful, the Word was faithful. The message was true and powerful.

When Jonah delivered the message of judgment to Nineveh, the people were profoundly affected. They all repented before God, from the king on down to the least important, in sackcloth and ashes. They mourned before God because of their evil deeds; they repented because of their sins. We can rejoice in the power of the Word of God. We can rejoice as we read how these people changed their ways.

God changed His plan, and this upset Jonah. Jonah was troubled that God seemed to have changed His mind. He expected God to be faithful. He expected God to be permanent, unchangeable. Jonah had the message from God, "In forty days Nineveh shall be destroyed," and that was the message he had preached, a message so powerful that it drastically affected the people. Then, when the people changed, God did not destroy the city. And that upset Jonah. We, like Jonah, are to learn from this that God is quick to forgive. We can praise His name for this.

Another general truth that Jonah was to learn is that God is compassionate. We are reminded of these wonderful words from Psalm 103:

> The Lord is merciful and gracious, slow to anger, and plente-
> ous in mercy. He will not always chide: neither will he keep his
> anger for ever. He hath not dealt with us after our sins; nor
> rewarded us according to our iniquities. For as the heaven is
> high above the earth, so great is his mercy toward them that
> fear him. As far as the east is from the west, so far hath he
> removed our transgressions from us. Like as a father pitieth his
> children, so the Lord pitieth them that fear him. For he
> knoweth our frame; he remembereth that we are dust (Ps.
> 103:8–14).

This is wonderful! God is compassionate. He has great mercy. And here is a very important thing to learn: the heart has reasons the mind knows nothing of. It is far more important to go by the heart than to go by our own thinking.

Another truth Jonah was to learn is that God is not bound. Actually God is consistent and faithful. He may not perform His will in the same way each day. We do know, however, that God cannot lie, and He is holy and just and true. He will not condone sin; He has purer eyes than to behold evil. The one simple statement is made that God cannot lie. But when it comes to acting out His will, according as He pleases, no-body can draw up any pattern for God. There is no one who can lay out the ground rules by which God is going to have to move. No situation and no person is ever out of reach of His mercy. He can deal with us regardless of what we have done. Jonah needed to learn these things, and looking over his shoulder, we can learn so much.

LESSONS FOR US

We are studying the Book of Jonah in the Old Testament for spiritual guidance for us as Christians. The Old Testament was written for our sake. If we should gain the impression that the Old Testament is a series of historical documents for their own sake, we would be missing its whole truth and purpose. Peter makes it clear:

> Of which salvation the prophets have inquired and searched
> diligently, who prophesied of the grace that should come unto
> you: searching what, or what manner of time the Spirit of
> Christ which was in them did signify, when it testified be-

forehand the sufferings of Christ, and the glory that should
follow. Unto whom it was revealed, that not unto themselves,
but unto us they did minister the things, which are now reported unto you by them that have preached the gospel unto
you with the Holy Ghost sent down from heaven; which things
the angels desire to look into (1 Peter 1:10–12).

Notice the words of the apostle Paul in writing to the Corin-
thians. He has just been writing about the exodus of Israel as
recorded in the Old Testament. He wrote "Now these things
[the Exodus events] were our examples, to the intent we
should not lust after evil things, as they also lusted" (1 Cor.
10:6). Also: "Now all these things happened unto them for
examples: and they are written for our admonition, upon
whom the ends of the world are come" (1 Cor. 10:11). Could it
be any plainer than this? These experiences happened to
them for examples, and they were written down for us.
Another passage, Romans 15:4, reads: "For whatsoever things
were written aforetime [that is, in Old Testament time] were
written for our learning, that we through patience and comfort of the scriptures might have hope." What can we say
more clearly than this? The Old Testament was written for us.
I do not think a person can be very intelligent about studying
the Bible and seeking the truth of Scripture and fail to study
the Old Testament. Those things were written for us.

Jonah is such a book. It is included in the list of the Minor
Prophets. It is a small book. But notice that this book is not
about Nineveh; we are not told much beyond the fact that it
was a wicked city. Nor is the book about Jonah; he is the
principal character, but there are no details about him as a
person. The Book of Jonah is about God and His dealing with
His people and with His servant. Jonah can be taken as typical
of any believer, and Nineveh is typical of the unbeliever.

We can learn several important truths from the Book of
Jonah. First, God wants His message taken to Nineveh, for
He cares about Nineveh. Sometimes it is felt that we who
preach about the Christian life have no interest in other
people. Oh no! The truth of the matter is, we are involved in a
great mission to other people. There is an unfinished job on
the face of the earth. Christians are to tell the world about
Jesus Christ. This is our commission.

God cares about unbelievers. There are men, women, and children all over the world suffering from just living here. It is hard to live in this world. The frustration, the troubles, and the hurt make life miserable and hard. But God cares. He sent His Son to die for us. He sent His believers to go out and tell the message of salvation. It is an unfinished job that needs to be done. God cares about the unbelieving world.

Now it is the nature of God that He cannot overlook the sin of unbelievers. But He can take care of their sin. Christ Jesus died for sinners. This is the truth He wants the world to know. God has no pleasure in the death of the wicked.

God sent His Son into the world to become incarnate as Jesus of Nazareth, and in Him are all the promises of God "yea and amen." Jesus is the express image of God. He said, "I am the way, the truth, and the life; no man cometh unto the Father, but by me" (John 14:6). God has revealed the truth in Jesus Christ, and that message is to be taken to the ends of the earth.

> Go ye therefore, and teach all nations, baptizing them in the name of the Father, and of the Son, and of the Holy Ghost: teaching them to observe all things whatsoever I have commanded you: and, lo, I am with you always, even unto the end of the world. Amen (Matt. 28:19–20).

This is what God wants done even to this day. The message of God's saving grace must be taken around the world and across the street. The glorious message should be taken into our homes and to our children.

God wants every human being on earth to be told that the ways of sin are abominable in His sight. "The soul that sinneth, it shall die." But every person should also be told that "whosoever will may come; . . . whosoever cometh he will in no wise cast out."

It was a notorious thing that Israel accepted the status of God's chosen people and then rejected their mission. They failed to tell anyone else. That never was intended. Jonah serves as an example; he was sent out to a Gentile city.

Let us not be too critical of Israel of old times. Let us look at ourselves and the church of today. Those of us who are real believers rejoice in our church. We may feel our own denomination is probably the best one. Yet it is an amazing thing how people can gather in one congregation and shun all others.

God wants the message taken to the unbelieving, to the blind, the ignorant, the lame, the halt. They could be saved. They could be healed. God is not pleased with our attitude if we fail to take the message. Sometimes my heart hurts when I listen to what is said in public today and the general common acceptance of the idea that times are different, times have changed, and things that our forefathers would not permit, we allow today. This permissiveness—wait a minute! It is not up to us to decide what will and will not be all right. God is the Judge, and the Law of God is eternal—far more enduring than the stars in heaven. God has showed us where He stands. People need to be told. They may not listen, but they need to be told.

So the first thing we can learn from Jonah is that a message needs to go to "Nineveh."

Secondly, as in the case of Jonah, each believer's individual assignment will be given to him. By the word "given," I mean that it will not be his own idea. No, the person will receive his call from God. He wants us to work with Him. The person's response will be primarily a matter of obedience!

It is as though I were walking alongside a canal and saw a four-year-old child stumble and fall into the water. Whose business is it to get the child out? Mine. Why? I was there. It is not my child—but that makes no difference. A child is drowning: that is my business!

When the Good Samaritan came along the road and saw a man in the ditch, he did not know who he was. He did not know the man's name or his pedigree. The man was hurt. That man was in trouble, and that man was the Samaritan's business. The Samaritan went over and tended to the job. Each person has a call from God. It is right there at hand, and our commission is "whatsoever your hand findeth to do, do it with all thy might."

The next truth in Jonah appears to be that disobedience brings chastisement. Even if the believer is unaware of what God wants him to do, he should be careful. God will stop him in his tracks. God is too faithful to let him go on with his foolishness.

It is surprising how easily we can miss the very things that we ought to be doing for God. God is faithful, but He does not strike us dead. Rather, He has ways of bringing things to pass. In Jonah's case we recall that God brought up the storm and had Jonah cast into the sea. God brought up the fish and had Jonah swallowed. He stopped Jonah in his tracks. Disobedience brings chastisement.

This is noted in Hebrews.

> And ye have forgotten the exhortation which speaketh unto you as unto children, My son, despise not thou the chastening of the Lord, nor faint when thou art rebuked of him: for whom the Lord loveth he chasteneth, and scourgeth every son whom he receiveth (Heb. 12:5–6).

This is something that we can learn from Jonah. When a person is being chastised, the way to God through repentance is always open. A person can always come to God. Even if the person is at fault, he can turn to God. Even if a person is in distress and cannot see a way out of his crisis, he can look up!

This is a marvelous truth. Praying should include praise, thanksgiving, and commital. If we are in deep trouble, we can cry out to God and praise Him. Consider how great He is. Thank Him for what He has done. Trust Him. Commit ourselves for service. "I will from henceforth do His will." This should always be included in prayer. Praying is never a matter of asking God for a great advantage so that one can go out and do as he pleases. In Christ, a person can be restored.

However, as in Jonah, the assignment may not be changed. If the believer failed to witness to his neighbor earlier, he may need to go and talk to him now.

What of the parent who has ignored or neglected his children and has failed to tell them about the Lord? A parent can humbly call on God and be set free. Now what? He should go, talk with his children. The assignment is not changed. That is what he was and is supposed to do. Obedience can replace disobedience. We can be changed completely. "Once you were blind, now you can see."

The Word of God is powerful. Jonah told the people in Nineveh what God said, and they changed their ways. And so it is with a believer's witness today. We should set it before the person. We should not take time to "justify" things. We do not know enough. We could not justify it if we tried. So we should not argue. If a person is not willing to see, we can't show him. We must set out the truth before them. God can show it to him. The Holy Spirit can do so. God's Word is powerful. Simply say it: Christ Jesus came into the world to seek and to save the lost. He is the Son of God who came to give His life a ransom for many. He died for others; He died for you. We can tell them that. We can tell them that we have a living Lord in heaven interceding on our behalf. We can tell them of the exhilarating joy that comes from belonging to God and knowing that we are going to heaven.

I remember one of our farmer neighbors said to me, "Manford, I understand that you feel that you are sure you are going to heaven." I said, "Yes, sir!" He said, "What makes you so sure?" I replied, "The Lord told me. I have it in His Word." Then he said, "You must think you are pretty good." When he said that, my blood ran cold. I said, "Oh no. I am not good. He is good." I remember how that man just looked at me. And then I tried to tell him. "I'm not any better than you are. It isn't because I think I am better than other people. It is because I think Christ Jesus is wonderful. 'Where sin abounds, grace does much more abound.'" God's Word is powerful. Tell it! God is quick to forgive.

We should never forget that when the wicked city of Nineveh repented, God forgave. That day, right then. The people were wrong. They confessed their sins. Immediately God received them. At once He forgave them. God is quick to forgive.

God is meek, long suffering, patient with His willful servant. We consider all He did for Jonah, and then Jonah criticized God for being kind to those Ninevites. To Jonah, God seemed to change His mind. God never explained that to Jonah. He showed Jonah He cares about the lost. God is not willing that any should perish, but that all should come to repentance and to everlasting life.

MICAH

† † †

WE NOW CONSIDER the prophet Micah, one of four prophets who preached in one generation in Israel. We have studied Hosea and Amos already; now we consider Micah; the other one of the four is Isaiah. These four preachers were contemporary with one another.

From the way in which he speaks and from the things he talks about, we perceive that Micah lived his life among the common people. He came from a little village called Moresheth, which I understand is just about fifteen miles from where Amos was born.

As we look into the message of Micah, we do not find anything very different from what we considered so far. We should remind ourselves of the situation involving these preachers. They preached to God's people. Their message was given to believers. The prophets came to Israel to tell the people that despite their relationship with God, they were becoming careless.

In the first three chapters of Micah the general theme is something like this: the immediate prospect for Israel is the judgment of God. God will bring judgment down upon His people because of their sin.

Hear, all ye people; hearken, O earth, and all that therein is:
and let the Lord God be witness against you, the Lord from his
holy temple. For, behold, the Lord cometh forth out of his
place, and will come down, and tread upon the high places of
the earth (Mic. 1:2–3).

This is a poetic way of saying that God will come from heaven
into this world and will tread upon it. He will walk upon it;
and when He comes, He comes to judge.

And the mountains shall be molten under him, and the valleys
shall be cleft, as wax before the fire, and as the waters that are
poured down a steep place (Mic. 1:4).

When God comes, things will really be brought into judgment, and will be shattered by His presence.

For the transgression of Jacob is all this, and for the sins of the
house of Israel. What is the transgression of Jacob? is it not
Samaria? and what are the high places of Judah? are they not
Jerusalem? (Mic. 1:5).

Samaria was a capital city. So was Jerusalem. These cities
were the seats of government for the northern and southern
kingdoms respectively. Jerusalem was also where the temple
was. Micah raised the question: "What is the transgression of
Jacob?" Where did Jacob really go wrong? In our day and
time this would be like saying, "Where are God's people
really at fault?" Micah pointed to the leadership, the capital
cities of the country, the head men. He also pointed to the
altars where the leaders gave false worship. Where in Judah
was this deviation, this turning from God? Was it not Jerusalem? This city was the very center of national life for the
southern kingdom. Micah pointed out that the reason why
God's people were getting careless was because of their leaders. This is as much as to say that the reason why the congregation of one of our churches today is not spiritual is because
of the preachers and the elders and the deacons.

Therefore I will make Samaria as a heap of the field, and as
plantings of a vineyard: and I will pour down the stones thereof
into the valley, and I will discover the foundations thereof. And
all the graven images thereof shall be beaten to pieces, and all
the hires thereof shall be burned with the fire, and all the idols
thereof will I lay desolate: for she gathered it of the hire of a
harlot, and they shall return to the hire of a harlot (Mic. 1:6–7).

This is poetic language, and in connection with that we may remember Hosea. The prophets always held the idea that to describe Israel as being unfaithful to God, they should use the figure of a wife being unfaithful to her husband. When we see this picture here and note the reference to adultery or to harlotry, we see in these inelegant and unpleasant words that the prophets were pointing their finger at spiritual defection from God. This is the main thing they were concerned about.

> Therefore I will wail and howl, I will go stripped and naked: I will make a wailing like the dragons, and mourning as the owls. For her wound is incurable; for it is come unto Judah; he is come unto the gate of my people, even to Jerusalem (Mic. 1:8–9).

Micah said, "I personally will be greatly distressed, and I will be bereft in my soul, because of the misery and the judgment that is going to come on my people." Micah started out his whole message by saying to God's people, "God is going to judge this place. God is going to judge you people. He is going to judge you because you have not been faithful. And the reason you have not been faithful is because your leaders have not been faithful."

Then Micah made an interesting point when he said, "Declare ye it not at Gath, weep ye not at all" (Mic. 1:10). Gath was the big city of the Philistines, the enemies of God's people. So this is Micah's way of saying God will judge the church. God's own people will be judged of Him. The problem of the church is the leaders. The ministers and the elders and the deacons and the stewards are causing the trouble. "My heart is desolate: I just feel terrible. . . . I will wail and howl," for God will certainly chasten His people. But Micah cautions the people of Israel not to tell the unbelievers about it. Don't tell unbelieving people about this thing. Publish it not in Gath.

This is something that every one of us should take to heart for ourselves. Scarcely anyone criticizes the Christian church as much as the people who are in it. We are as quick as anybody to find fault with ourselves, but we ought to be very careful. When we make derogatory comments, we should not give comfort to unbelievers.

Micah did not draw attention to cruder sins, but rather to

the peculiar sins of God's people. Persons who believe in God may be refined in their conduct. They do the kind of things that nice people do who are not right with God. As the children of Israel went to sleep at night they were thinking about how they were going to get ahead of someone else. On their beds at night they were planning what they would do the next day and how they could advance their own covetous schemes.

> Woe to them that devise iniquity, and work evil upon their beds! when the morning is light, they practice it, because it is in the power of their hand (Mic. 2:1).

We may ask what terrible things these people were going to do. What were they lying awake at night thinking about? Micah made it plain: they were figuring out how to get that piece of property; how to get ahold of that house or that business, how to crowd out some competitor.

> And they covet fields, and take them by violence; and houses, and take them away: so they oppress a man and his house, even a man and his heritage (Mic. 2:2).

This is what Micah found wrong with the people. They were dishonest. They were covetous. They were thinking about money all the time. Now there are many other kinds of wickedness. There is theft, and there is murder. There is adultery, and there is lying. But these people were not accused of all those kinds of things. They did not commit the violent crimes. As a minister of the Gospel I must confess that some church members practice some of the most refined sins you ever saw. We are just so nice we would not do anything crude or vulgar; but we are so crooked spiritually that nobody outside the church could top us. We are just too nice to do an ugly thing. But we are downright selfish and proud; we are vain and arrogant; and we are very irritable and very sensitive.

> Therefore thus saith the Lord; Behold, against this family do I devise an evil, from which ye shall not remove your necks; neither shall ye go haughtily: for this time is evil. In that day shall one take up a parable against you, and lament with a doleful lamentation, and say, We be utterly spoiled (Mic. 2:3–4).

This passage uses the English word "spoil" in a way that is unfamiliar to us today. Ordinarily we think of "spoiling" as in the case of a spoiled child, or perhaps we think of a spoiled cake, or something that has gone bad. But this word "spoil" has military significance. The contemporary English word would be "despoil." We have become utterly impoverished —despoiled. We have been robbed. We have lost. This doleful lamentation is caused by our covetousness, by our being overly interested in worldly things, by our going after money. We are utterly despoiled in spiritual things. We have gone out after money, but our hearts are empty. This is what Micah meant.

> Prophesy ye not, say they to them that prophesy: they shall not
> prophesy to them, that they shall not take shame (Mic. 2:6).

Micah chose a rather awkward way of expressing his point, but he meant to say that one characteristic of these people is that they did not want any preacher to tell them the truth. They wanted the preacher to preach nice things. They did not want the preacher to tell them how it really was because he would make them uncomfortable. This was their second kind of sin. The first is that they were deliberately covetous, trying to get ahead of other people. The second is that there was an unwillingness to heed God's Word. If we are not willing for a preacher to show us our spiritual emptiness, the result is our loss. Thus we will be despoiled.

> O thou that art named the house of Jacob, is the spirit of the
> Lord straitened? are these his doings? do not my words do
> good to him that walketh uprightly? (Mic. 2:7).

Micah was saying, "Have you narrowed down the Spirit of the Lord? Don't you think God could bless you?" This is the way Micah would preach to a church that had regular church services but no spiritual power. If a church held regular services, with members going through the usual activities in the congregation but without spiritual power, then in calling on people to pray, nobody would want to pray. When time came to sing, nobody would want to sing. When the time came to read Scripture, nobody would open a Bible. They do not have the faith they could have. They are not sure about things; they are not even sure about God. They are not sure about the resurrection; they are not sure about eternal life; they are not sure about heaven. They do not even know whether they are saved. Micah would ask in such a situation, "Is that the way God works? Is the Spirit of the Lord really straitened? Have you narrowed Him down? Has God lost His power?" "Do not my words do good to him that walketh uprightly?" is the way Micah preached to the people.

> Even of late my people is risen up as an enemy: ye pull off the robe with the garment from them that pass by securely as men averse from war. The women of my people have ye cast out from their pleasant houses; from their children have ye taken away my glory for ever (Mic. 2:8–9).

These words are a rather roundabout way of saying that the people have been robbed of their spiritual benefits and blessings.

> Arise ye, and depart; for this is not your rest: because it is polluted, it shall destroy you, even with a sore destruction. If a man walking in the spirit and falsehood do lie, saying, I will prophesy unto thee of wine and of strong drink: he shall even be the prophet of this people (Mic. 2:10–11).

Micah wrote that there was a readiness among the people to listen to empty preaching. They did not want to hear real down-to-earth Gospel preaching. When Micah said, "If a man walking in the spirit and falsehood do lie," he meant to say that if a man made pretense in the pulpit and did not really mean what he was saying, but talked about a lot of things he really did not care for in his own heart, the people would listen. If he were to say, "I will prophesy unto thee of wine and of strong drink"—that is, preaching after he had taken a stimulant—the people would accept him. There have been preachers who would take a drink of liquor so they would be loosened up to speak. Nevertheless, "wine and strong drink" does not necessarily mean the man has to take spirits or liquors; rather, it means he derives his inspiration from natural things.

Some things in this world are exciting to talk about. A person could mention some current political crisis and in about ten sentences have half his audience in great excitement. But in discussing political things that really arouse them we certainly would not remember anything about Micah. And we might not remember anything about God, but we would be sure to remember the sensational things the preacher talked about. "Wine and strong drink" in preaching is when the preacher is drawing his inspiration from human, natural, earthly things.

We might wonder what a preacher could do. Paul expressed it in one sentence in Ephesians. "And be not drunk with wine, wherein is excess; but be filled with the Spirit" (Eph. 5:18). These two things are put together in one sentence because their operations are similar. In the ministry there is a choice to be made. In his preaching is a minister to lay hold on those things to which people will naturally listen, or will he lay hold on God so that the things he says sink right into the heart of his hearers and reveal the things of God?

In chapter 3 Micah focuses more closely on the leaders. He mentions three different kinds of people in this chapter. In the first four verses Micah speaks of the leaders who have done wrong.

> And I said, Hear, I pray you, O heads of Jacob, and ye princes of the house of Israel; Is it not for you to know judgment? Who hate the good, and love the evil; who pluck off their skin from off them, and their flesh from off their bones; who also eat the flesh of my people, and flay their skin from off them; and they break their bones, and chop them in pieces, as for the pot, and as flesh within the caldron (Mic. 3:1–3).

This is very rough language to express Micah's idea that the leaders exploited the people to their own advantage. They conducted themselves in places of leadership for self-benefit. But God judged them to be evil.

> Then shall they cry unto the Lord, but he will not hear them: he will even hide his face from them at that time, as they have behaved themselves ill in their doings (Mic. 3:4).

Micah points out that the leaders of God's people have done wrong, so God will not hear their prayer.

> Thus saith the Lord concerning the prophets that make my people err, that bite with their teeth, and cry, Peace (Mic. 3:5).

There are leaders who do things to provoke us and then say, "Let us all be friends." First they go out and do the very things to which we are opposed, the very things we do not want. When they have done what they will, then they say,

"What we want is that all should love one another. Now let us all love one another." They bite with their teeth. And then they say, "Peace, peace." When we are ready to retaliate, they say, "We all ought to love one another."

Micah wrote further about these leaders that "he that putteth not into their mouths, they even prepare war against him." He meant by this that if anyone did not feed such a leader well, that leader was ready to prepare war against him. Anyone who did not support their plans and projects, and who did not contribute to what they were doing, they were against him. Micah announced about such leaders: "Therefore night shall be unto you, that ye shall not have a vision." When preachers have served their own purposes and preached peace insincerely, in a belligerent mood, the result will be that night comes upon the people.

> Then shall the seers be ashamed, and the diviners confounded: yea, they shall all cover their lips; for there is no answer of God (Mic. 3:7).

God will not be speaking through such leaders.

> But truly I am full of power by the spirit of the Lord, and of judgment, and of might, to declare unto Jacob his transgression, and to Israel his sin. Hear this, I pray you, ye heads of the house of Jacob, and princes of the house of Israel, that abhor judgment, and pervert all equity. They build up Zion with blood, and Jerusalem with iniquity. The heads thereof judge for reward, and the priests thereof teach for hire, and the prophets thereof divine for money: yet will they lean upon the Lord, and say, Is not the Lord among us? none evil can come upon us (Mic. 3:8–11).

Micah points out that every leader was in it for what he could get out of it. Micah was not so much an awful preacher—he was simply telling the truth. Micah was telling them the truth the way a person works who is trying to get old paint off a piece of furniture in order to refinish it. Micah was just really trying to get down to the original wood. He was trying to get through the veneer of superficial practices that the people had developed. He was trying to get down to the actual facts of their case. The prophet pointed out their selfish motives in saying, "The heads thereof judge for reward, and the priests thereof teach for hire, and the prophets thereof divine for money: yet will they lean upon the Lord, and say, Is not the Lord among us?" He was noting that, although they were acting out of self-interest, they would publicly say, "God is with us."

> Therefore shall Zion for your sake be plowed as a field, and Jerusalem shall become heaps, and the mountain of the house as the high places of the forest (Mic. 3:12).

In that country the cities were built of material much like clay. The houses were made of clay brick, and when those houses crumbled, they became dust heaps. "Zion for your sake be plowed as a field" means the whole city would be burned off and destroyed. Their enemies would just plow the rubble under. "And Jerusalem shall become heaps": mounds of ruins and rubbish.

In these first three chapters of Micah the immediate prospect is the judgment of God. In chapters 4 and 5 the sure future will see God's plan done. In chapter 4 Micah notes that God's leadership will rise to prominence and draw all men to it in obedience. This passage is much like Isaiah 2.

> But in the last days it shall come to pass, that the mountain of the house of the Lord shall be established in the top of the mountains, and it shall be exalted above the hills; and the people shall flow unto it. And many nations shall come, and say, Come, and let us go up to the mountain of the Lord, and to the house of the God of Jacob; and he will teach us of his ways, and we will walk in his paths: for the law shall go forth of Zion, and the word of the Lord from Jerusalem. And he shall judge among many people, and rebuke strong nations afar off; and they shall beat their swords into plowshares, and their spears into pruninghooks: nation shall not lift up a sword against nation, neither shall they learn war any more. But they shall sit every man under his vine and under his fig tree; and none shall make them afraid: for the mouth of the Lord of hosts hath spoken it (Mic. 4:1–4).

This is a wonderful picture of the peace that comes after the people of the world gather in God's house to learn His Word. God means that man shall have peace. God works toward that end. There is a simple prerequisite to having peace, and that is to get right with God. Let the human soul get right with God, and the human soul can have peace. Let the community get right with God, and the community can have peace. Let the whole world get right with God, and the whole world can have peace. And the way to get right with God is to come to the "mountain of the Lord"—His house. We must come to where the Word of God is taught, and listen to it, and let the Word of God instruct us. And if we will let the Word of God instruct us, then we will turn from war to peace.

Today there are many people talking peace, in the same way that one of the prophets says, "Peace, peace, when there is no peace." Many people talk about peace as though peace were something we could have in ourselves alone. But we cannot have peace unless we get right with God.

> In that day, saith the Lord, will I assemble her that halteth, and I will gather her that is driven out, and her that I have afflicted; and I will make her that halted a remnant, and her that was cast far off a strong nation: and the Lord shall reign over them in mount Zion from henceforth, even for ever. And thou, O tower of the flock, the stronghold of the daughter of Zion, unto thee shall it come, even the first dominion; the kingdom shall come to the daughter of Jerusalem (Mic. 4:6–8).

At the end of verse 10 we read: "There the Lord shall redeem thee from the hand of thine enemies." We are told here that God's leadership will rise to prominence and draw all men to it in obedience.

In chapter 5 Micah reveals that God's will will be manifested by His Chosen One, the Messiah.

> But thou Bethlehem Ephratah, though thou be little among the thousands of Judah, yet out of thee shall he come forth unto me that is to be ruler in Israel' whose goings forth have been from of old, from everlasting (Mic. 5:2).

This is how the Word of God is going to be taught. Despite all this trouble present in Micah's own time—the incompetent and insincere leadership and resultant despoiling of the people and the coming judgment of God—the time will come when there will be a radical, positive change. Micah lifts the curtain of the future and says in effect: "But the day is coming, in the last days, when it will come to pass that the mountain of the Lord's house shall be raised up. People will come to it and will listen to the Word of God, and when they do, peace will come." Micah says this will come through the Chosen One, the Ruler, the Messiah, whom we know as Jesus Christ.

And he shall stand and feed in the strength of the Lord, in the
majesty of the name of the Lord his God; and they shall abide:
for now shall he be great unto the ends of the earth. And this
man shall be the peace, when the Assyrian shall come into our
land. . . . And the remnant of Jacob shall be in the midst of
many people as a dew from the Lord, as the showers upon the
grass, that tarrieth not for man, nor waiteth for the sons of men.
And the remnant of Jacob shall be among the Gentiles in the
midst of many people as a lion among the beasts of the forest
(Mic. 5:4–8).

After this, Micah announces judgment upon the pagan
people. God is going to judge those people, just as in the first
three chapters He judged His own. Now in chapters 4 and 5
Micah reveals the promise of God. God is going to lead His
people back to Himself. In view of such judgment and such
promise, Israel could reasonably decide to walk in the ways of
God. That is what Micah was seeking to bring to pass by his
preaching. Micah wanted God's people to get the idea that
they reliably could turn to Him.

Hear ye now what the Lord saith; Arise, contend thou before
the mountains, and let the hills hear thy voice. Hear ye, O
mountains, the Lord's controversy, and ye strong foundations
of the earth: for the Lord hath a controversy with his people,
and he will plead with Israel. O my people, what have I done
unto thee? and wherein have I wearied thee? testify against me
(Mic. 6:1–3).

Micah reveals God is challenging Israel to find any wrong in
what He did:

For I brought thee up out of the land of Egypt, and redeemed
thee out of the house of servants; and I sent before thee Moses,
Aaron, and Miriam (Mic. 6:4).

God had done visible works for them. They could have
trusted Him.

Wherewith shall I come before the Lord, and bow myself before the high God? shall I come before him with burnt offerings, with calves of a year old? Will the Lord be pleased with
thousands of rams, or with ten thousands of rivers of oil? shall I
give my first-born for my transgression, the fruit of my body for
the sin of my soul? He hath showed thee, O man, what is good;
and what doth the Lord require of thee, but to do justly, and to
love mercy, and to walk humbly with thy God? (Mic. 6:6–8).

Verse 8, in which the prophet says, "What doth the Lord require of thee, but to do justly, and to love mercy, and to walk humbly with thy God?" does not contradict Acts 16:30–31: "Sirs, what must I do to be saved? And they said, Believe on the Lord Jesus Christ, and thou shalt be saved, and thy house." One is not a contradiction of the other. Verse 8 is actually speaking to Christian people, to believers. This is what Micah says to Christian people who ask, "What am I as a believing person to do to be acceptable in the sight of God? I who believe in God and trust in God—what does God require of me? Shall I bring a sacrifice?" Back in those days it was "Shall I come before Him with burnt offerings. . . ?"

If we as believers in Christ come before God, what does He want from us? Shall we continually bring the cross of Calvary before Him? Shall we continually say to Him 'Christ Jesus died for our sins'? If we say that over and over and over again and do nothing more further than that, it is folly. When we do what God wants, we bring the cross, we bring the sacrifices.

Micah never meant that the people should not bring the calves, or the rams, or the oil. But just bringing those things is not enough. When we come before the Lord and offer up Calvary's cross, that is not enough. God looks on our hearts. He wants us to do justly, to love mercy, and to walk humbly with Him. He wants us genuinely and sincerely to yield to Him. "A body hast thou prepared for me: lo, I come to do thy will, O God." This is what God wants to hear from the Christian.

God's people have been bought and paid for. They are not their own. They are bought with a price. Therefore they should glorify God in their body and in their spirit, which are God's. This is what brings sincerity and truth into a church situation and into a personal Christian life. We do bring Calvary's cross. We do bring the blood of the Lord Jesus Christ in regard to our sins. But the hands that bring this sacrifice to God are yielded hands. The believer says, "Here I am; do with me as you will."

This is the message of all the prophets: "Repent." It involves deeply, inwardly, sincerely changing our ways before God in line with our faith, in line with what we actually believe about God. When John the Baptist preached the necessity of repentance, he did not mean that people should not bring sacrifices, but rather, when they did bring sacrifices, they were to bring them from the heart. They were to really mean it.

This means that as far as our churches are concerned, it is not merely religious services that God wants. Certainly believers come to church to sing hymns and read the Bible. We join in prayer and listen to the Word. We do all these things. But God looks on the heart. What God wants out of us is that we practice justice; that we love mercy—His mercy toward us and our mercy toward other people. We are to walk humbly with our God. We are to be yielded in the will of God. This is the real truth of a Christian's life, the real character of a godly life, according to Micah.

In chapters 6 and 7 Micah describes something more of the sinfulness of the people. Because of their dishonesty and deceit, Micah told them, God will bring judgment in the form of chronic dissatisfaction. They will never be satisfied.

> Thou shalt eat, but not be satisfied; . . . and thou shalt take hold, but shalt not deliver. . . . Thou shalt sow, but thou shalt not reap; thou shalt tread the olives, but thou shalt not anoint thee with oil; and sweet wine, but shalt not drink wine (Mic. 6:14–15).

Such would be the consequence of the wickedness among these people.

In chapter 7 it is stated that wickedness is general—all-encompassing and pervasive. There is none upright at all.

> The good man is perished out of the earth: and there is none upright among men. . . . The best of them is as a brier: the most upright is sharper than a thorn hedge. . . . Trust ye not in a friend, put ye not confidence in a guide: keep the doors of thy mouth from her that lieth in thy bosom (Mic. 7:2–5).

There was such widespread unfaithfulness in the time of Micah that no one could be trusted. When people are unsettled and unfaithful to God, they are unfaithful to each other. When people do not "play square" with God, they will not play square with anybody.

> Notwithstanding the land shall be desolate because of them that dwell therein, for the fruit of their doings (Mic. 7:13).

The judgment will come down upon the whole of the country because of what the people have done.

> Feed thy people with thy rod, the flock of thine heritage, which dwell solitarily in the wood, in the midst of Carmel: let them feed in Bashan and Gilead, as in the days of old. According to the days of thy coming out of the land of Egypt will I show unto him marvelous things (Mic. 7:14–15).

Coming out of the land of Egypt was the beginning of a crucial phase in the history of God's people. It was something like a conversion experience. A contemporary way of expressing this would be, "I will be with him the way I was at the time he was converted. Just the way it was with him at the beginning of his life in Christ, that is the way I am going to bring it to him."

> The nations shall see and be confounded at all their might: they shall lay their hand upon their mouth, their ears shall be deaf (Mic. 7:16).

People will be amazed at what God will do with His people.

And then Micah's message ends. This stern preacher—this sharp-tongued man who bore down on the sins of the people and ripped, as it were, all the trappings from the men in high places, showing them up for the negligent and wayward men that they were—now comes to this conclusion:

> Who is a God like unto thee, that pardoneth iniquity, and passeth by the transgression of the remnant of his heritage? he retaineth not his anger for ever, because he delighteth in mercy (Mic. 7:18).

This is the preacher who has pronounced judgment, yet he ends his message by emphasizing the fact that God pardons iniquity and passes by the transgression.

> He will turn again, he will have compassion upon us; he will subdue our iniquities; and thou wilt cast all their sins into the depths of the sea. Thou wilt perform the truth to Jacob, and the mercy to Abraham, which thou hast sworn unto our fathers from the days of old (Mic. 7:19–20).

This preacher lived in a day when God's people had become wayward, when they had turned in their hearts away from God. And having a heavy message to preach, telling them that "just as surely as you turn from God, God will have to judge you," so he came at the end to say, "And yet God will bring His will to pass among you, and He will pardon you and will cleanse you and will keep you."

One of the wonderful things about dealing with God is this: God may chasten us, but He will not destroy us. God may humble us, but He will not wipe us out. God may judge us, but He will never cast us off. "He that hath begun a good work in you will complete it."

The day we gave our hearts to God, He gave Himself to us. We may be unfaithful; He will not be unfaithful.

But we could have so much more blessing if we would walk with Him while we live in this world. It would be so much happier and so much more glorious if while we live in this world, we would walk humbly with our God.

NAHUM

† † †

NAHUM IS THE second book among the Minor Prophets that deals with Nineveh. Nineveh was the capital city of Assyria and came into the affairs of God's people as the instrument in the providence of God which destroyed Israel, the northern kingdom. It is a classic example of the ways of God in which He will use unbelieving people to accomplish His purpose.

God is concerned for His people. He wants to bless them, but His blessing can be received only by humble, repentant souls. When God's people become vain and proud, and in their arrogance depart from the way of God, God sends prophets to preach His call to His people to return to Him. When they persist in their willful disobedience, God raises up enemies who will harass them until they repent and turn to Him.

The longsuffering of God can be ignored, and His people can become incorrigible in their indifference and disobedience to Him. This happened in the case of the northern kingdom first. When Israel had departed from God beyond "the point of no return," He raised up a pagan nation, Assyria, who would come from the north and destroy the kingdom.

Although Assyria did the will of God in destroying Israel,

they did so in unbelief. They had no thought of doing God's will. They were pursuing their own selfish ends when they cruelly destroyed Israel without mercy.

Then God wanted to show His sovereignty by destroying Nineveh for the very action by which they had unwittingly done His will. Just as they had been merciless in their conquest of Israel, so God would destroy them without mercy. Assyria attacked Judah, the southern kingdom, but God protected Judah so that the Assyrians were turned back.

Nahum preached in Judah. The message of this book was focused on Nineveh, but seems to have been delivered in Judah so that God's people might have the comfort of knowing their enemy would be destroyed while at the same time they would be warned against disobedience before God.

One aspect of spiritual truth often ignored, if not forgotten, is expressed this way in the New Testament:

> Vengeance belongeth unto me, I will recompense, saith the Lord . . . It is a fearful thing to fall into the hands of the living God (Heb. 10:30–31).

The longsuffering of God should not be misunderstood as slackness. "God is angry with the wicked every day" (Ps. 7:11). Scripture also says, "My spirit shall not always strive with man" (Gen. 6:3). In the Book of Nahum there is a description of the thorough destruction God will bring upon the wicked.

> With an overrunning flood he will make an utter end of the place thereof, and darkness shall pursue his enemies. . . . And the Lord hath given a commandment concerning thee, that no more of thy name be sown: . . . for thou art vile (Nah. 1:8, 14).

The apostle Paul also describes such final judgment:

> Seeing it is a righteous thing with God to recompense tribulation to them that trouble you; and to you who are troubled rest with us, when the Lord Jesus shall be revealed from heaven with his mighty angels, in flaming fire taking vengeance on them that know not God, and that obey not the gospel of our Lord Jesus Christ: who shall be punished with everlasting destruction from the presence of the Lord, and from the glory of his power (2 Thess. 1:6–9).

The great English expositor G. Campbell Morgan saw in this book three aspects of vengeance:

The prophecy of Nahum gives a definite impression as to what it means "to fall into the hands of the living God." Popular emphasis on the grace of God has doubtless given the widespread impression that God will tolerate any sort of wrongdoing. We note that Paul did say on Mars Hill, "The times of this ignorance God winked at," and this may have contributed to the loose expectation that God will overlook anything if only the person involved is sorry for his sin. In any case there need be no question but that the prevailing notion among men who hear the Gospel message today are disposed to think that God will not condemn anyone to destruction and punishment.

From such a point of view, the Book of Nahum seems quite out of line with what is held to be the message of the Gospel. In this book the prophet describes the dire action of God in "taking vengeance" upon such as have ignored Him. But it is right at this point that Nahum supplies a needed corrective to the popular fallacy.

> God is jealous, and the Lord revengeth; the Lord revengeth and is furious; . . . Who can stand before his indignation? and who can abide in the fierceness of his anger? his fury is poured out like fire, and the rocks are thrown down by him (Nah. 1:2, 6).

Jeremiah wrote in a similar vein of a time when Israel had been misled by false prophets.

> They have healed also the hurt of the daughter of my people slightly, saying, Peace, peace; when there is no peace (Jer. 6:14).

He went on to report the final result:

> We looked for peace, but no good came; and for a time of health, and behold trouble! (Jer. 8:15).

It is possible that some will cherish the thought that Jesus of Nazareth would never share in any such destructive punishment of the wicked, but this would require either ignorance or disbelief of the plain word of Scripture. In warning against offending "one of the little ones who believe in me" Jesus of Nazareth announced plainly that for such a person

> it were better for him that a millstone were hanged about his neck, and that he were drowned in the depth of the sea (Matt. 18:6).

Pursuing the thought further, Jesus announced openly:

> Woe unto the world because of offenses! for it must needs be that offenses come; but woe to that man by whom the offense cometh! Wherefore if thy hand or thy foot offend thee, cut them off, and cast them from thee: it is better for thee to enter into life halt or maimed, rather than having two hands or two feet to be cast into everlasting fire. And if thine eye offend thee, pluck it out, and cast it from thee: it is better for thee to enter into life with one eye, rather than having two eyes to be cast into hell fire. Take heed that ye despise not one of these little ones; for I say unto you, That in heaven their angels do always behold the face of my Father which is in heaven (Matt. 18:7–10).

The fate of Nineveh may be seen as the fate of the wicked, so we are thus reminded of the eternal purpose of God to destroy the unbelieving and the disobedient. Nothing that Jesus Christ has done will change this settled purpose of God to vindicate the righteous and to wreak vengeance upon the ungodly. Paul reminded the Christians at Rome: "Vengeance is mine; I will repay, saith the Lord" (Rom. 12:19).

In a letter to the Thessalonians Paul makes it painfully clear that the second coming of Christ is the time when God will act in judgment by destroying utterly "them that know not God, and that obey not the gospel of our Lord Jesus Christ" (2 Thess. 1:8–9).

Announcing the doom of Nineveh, Nahum leaves no room for hope of any relenting on God's part. In this case "the cup of the Amorites" was full.

Yet here and there Nahum inserts a gracious word of promise to God's people. Judgment will fall upon the enemies of God, but it shall not come upon His own!

> The Lord is good, a stronghold in the day of trouble; and he knoweth them that trust in him (Nah. 1:7).

And again Nahum writes:

> Behold upon the mountains the feet of him that bringeth good
> tidings, that publisheth peace! O Judah, keep thy solemn
> feasts, perform thy vows: for the wicked shall no more pass
> through thee; he is utterly cut off (Nah. 1:15).

But the dead weight of the message of final judgment, vengeance, and retribution cannot be misunderstood.

HABAKKUK

† † †

THE MESSAGE OF Habakkuk is an interpretation of the dilemma of a believing man in an ungodly world where sin abounds. Habakkuk was a believing person whose concern was the problem of evil. Why does the holy God allow evil to go on? If God is almighty—and He is; and if God is good—and He is: why does God let the righteous die? This was the problem troubling Habakkuk.

This is also the problem encountered in the life of Job. "I did everything I knew how to do" said Job. "I did my very best to avoid doing anything that would bring on me the judgment of God. I feared this very thing, that I would fall into trouble. I took every precaution I possibly could and it happened to me anyway. Why did it happen to me?"

Psalm 73 follows the same line of thought. Jeremiah raised the same question. Habakkuk, preaching years later, foresaw the Chaldeans invading. The Chaldeans were pagans. They were vicious, powerful, ruthless, cruel, evil people coming in to devastate the people of God. Habakkuk could see it was going to happen, and it troubled him.

> O Lord, how long shall I cry, and thou wilt not hear! even cry
> out unto thee of violence, and thou wilt not save! Why dost
> thou show me iniquity, and cause me to behold grievance? for

> spoiling and violence are before me: and there are that raise up
> strife and contention (Hab. 1:2–3).

Habakkuk said in effect: "It just bothers me. God is almighty and powerful: He is our God. Trouble and evil are rampant and are gaining ground. I can't figure it out." Because these things are so, Habakkuk pointed out:

> Therefore the law is slacked, and judgment doth never go
> forth: for the wicked doth compass about the righteous; there-
> fore wrong judgment proceedeth (Hab. 1:4).

People get discouraged to stand up for what is right and good. They see evil triumph and they grow weary. "For the wicked doth compass about the righteous." Like wrestlers the wicked put their arms around others and pull them down. Thus the wicked get the advantage over the righteous. "Therefore wrong judgment proceedeth." People get the wrong ideas. And Habakkuk saw all this.

It seems sometimes that for some of us who preach and for those of us who try to help other people understand the Lord, it would be so much simpler if the good people were rich and healthy and well, and all the wicked people were poor and miserable. But God has a way of screening us out. He has a way of sifting us. Sometimes a young person comes to the Lord full of exuberance and wants to commit himself to the Lord. He may sincerely want to walk with the Lord, but he has much in him that ought to be taken out of him. So God may lead him through a shrinking process.

God leads His servants through a screening or purging process. They may pass through experiences that seem to tear the very heart out of them. But this has to be done, because they have things in them that are not good. It is like weeding in the garden, or cutting the extra branches off a grapevine. It is pruning. Just as young trees need to be pruned, so the new believer in Christ needs to have this purging experience.

Christians who have understanding and mature knowledge about this should stand by other believers when they have trouble. Their trouble is not a sign that God is against them, nor is it an indication that God has turned His back on them. "For whom the Lord loveth he chasteneth, and scourgeth every son whom he receiveth" (Heb. 12:6). It is our ministry to interpret this to believers, to help them to understand it. Habakkuk had that responsibility. Habakkuk saw that the Chaldeans would invade the land.

> For, lo, I raise up the Chaldeans, that bitter and hasty nation, which shall march through the breadth of the land, to possess the dwelling places that are not theirs. They are terrible and dreadful: their judgment and their dignity shall proceed of themselves (Hab. 1:6-7).

Then he saw how the invading nation would change its attitude.

> Then shall his mind change, and he shall pass over, and offend, imputing this his power unto his god (Hab. 1:11).

The Chaldeans will come in and be victorious. Evil will mount up and overflow the situation. This caused a problem to the prophet:

> Art thou not from everlasting, O Lord my God, mine Holy One? we shall not die. O Lord, thou hast ordained them for judgment; and, O mighty God, thou hast established them for correction. Thou art of purer eyes than to behold evil, and canst not look on iniquity: wherefore lookest thou upon them that deal treacherously? (Hab. 1:12-13).

We can feel Habakkuk calling upon all that is within him and looking up into the face of God: "O God, thou art holy. O Lord, thou art righteous. And thou hast given us gracious promises and thou art against everything that is evil. How is it that you can let the wicked prevail as they do?"

> Wherefore lookest thou upon them that deal treacherously, and holdest thy tongue when the wicked devoureth the man that is more righteous than he? (Hab. 1:13).

This is the line of thought through the first chapter.

In chapter 2 Habakkuk said what he would do, which I believe is the proper procedure of a believing man.

> I will stand upon my watch, and set me upon the tower, and will watch to see what he will say unto me, and what I shall answer when I am reproved (Hab. 2:1).

Habakkuk suggests what is wise for any of us to do. When we have felt the problem Habakkuk felt, when our hearts are distressed because of the seeming triumph of wickedness, and it looks as though the evil were getting ahead—when it looks as if the people we know who are not right in the sight of God seem to get their way; when they connive and manage and scheme to get their own way—and we are about to be discouraged, the one thing we should do is to be quiet. We should close our mouths. We would be sure to say something foolish. We might say God does not care for us. We might say that God does not care what happens. So we should keep quiet. We should at least follow Habakkuk.

No matter what we are thinking, we should go aside some place and stay still and watch.

> And the Lord answered me, and said, Write the vision, and make it plain upon tables, that he may run that readeth it. For the vision is yet for an appointed time, but at the end it shall speak, and not lie: though it tarry, wait for it; because it will surely come, it will not tarry. Behold, his soul which is lifted up is not upright in him: but the just shall live by his faith (Hab. 2:2–4).

We should never forget this about the proud man. We should never for one moment think he is going to get away with it. About that man whose soul is lifted up—the proud man like those Chaldeans, the bitter and hasty nation that was traveling through and sweeping everything before it, ascribing all power to their god—about that man almighty God says: "Habakkuk, mark it down. Don't you ever forget it. That proud man is not going to get away with it. He is not upright." Then God gave the words that shine so brightly in the darkness: "The just shall live by his faith." This central truth is found here in Habakkuk. It was repeated again and again in Scripture, and it became the great truth of the Reformation: The just man—the man who is right in the sight of God— lives by his faith, not by his pride nor by his strength.

Then there is a description of what God will do with the wicked. The rest of chapter 2 is given to specific examples:

> Woe to him that coveteth an evil covetousness. . . .
>
> Woe unto him that buildeth a town with blood. . . .
>
> Woe unto him that giveth his neighbor drink, that puttest thy bottle to him, and makest him drunken also. . . .
>
> Woe unto him that saith to the wood, Awake; to the dumb stone, Arise (Hab. 2:9–19).

As surely as God is in heaven, His judgment will definitely come. It will not come at once. The believer is to wait for it.

It seems as though God in His great plan has a way of challenging faith. We may come in at the beginning and then have to wait with long patience for the victory which we are thoroughly assured will certainly come. Such is the insight and the understanding of the believer. The person who stands alone with God, who looks up into His face, has this problem in his heart: he feels the situation in the world the way it is; he knows about the wicked seeming to prosper: but he comes into the presence of God, looks up into God's face, and hears God speak right to him and tell him, "Don't you ever mistake it: the wicked, the proud, the folks who lift themselves up, are not going to get away with it." Only the person who trusts in God will be righteous in His sight.

Habakkuk experienced this truth, and he also gained that insight.

> O Lord, I have heard thy speech, and was afraid: O Lord, revive thy work in the midst of the years, in the midst of the years make known; in wrath remember mercy (Hab. 3:2).

This is the prayer of Habakkuk. So the wicked seem to triumph? It may seem so for a little while. But looking into the face of God, the believer sees the truth and can pray, "O Lord, revive us. We need stronger faith. We need the faith that will carry us through. We will have to wait for you to act and for that we need faith."

This is where revival comes in. We pray, "Revive the faith that we have, and have had in the past; and make us strong. In wrath, in the working out of thy great judgment upon this world the way in which thou wilt work it out, remember mercy. We need thee. We need thee now."

Habakkuk gives a great description of what God would do next in regard to His people and those who oppressed them.

> God came from Teman . . . and his brightness was as the light. . . . He stood, and measured the earth . . . (Hab. 3:3–6).

Then Habakkuk saw more specifically how God would act.

> Thou didst march through the land in indignation, thou didst thresh the heathen in anger. Thou wentest forth for the salva-

> tion of thy people, even for salvation with thine anointed; thou woundedst the head out of the house of the wicked. . . . Thou didst strike through with his staves the head of his villages. . . . Thou didst walk through the sea with thine horses. . . . (Hab. 3:12–15).

Habakkuk said that when he saw what God was going to do in judgment, "my belly trembled." That is to say his emotional being, his whole being, was shocked. He was stunned.

> When I heard, my belly trembled; my lips quivered at the voice: rottenness entered into my bones, and I trembled in myself, that I might rest in the day of trouble: when he cometh up unto the people, he will invade them with his troops (Hab. 3:16).

Just as surely as we see godlessness rampant—just as surely as we see sin and evil on the increase in the world—we can be very sure God will bring judgment down. Habakkuk said it frightened him when he thought of how God would deal with these who have been proud in His sight.

In the latter verses of the book, Habakkuk expresses the assurance of a believing man.

> Although the fig tree shall not blossom, neither shall fruit be in the vines; the labor of the olive shall fail, and the fields shall yield no meat; the flock shall be cut off from the fold, and there shall be no herd in the stalls: yet I will rejoice in the Lord, I will joy in the God of my salvation (Hab. 3:17–18).

Oh, what a wonderful thing it is to be lifted up this way in faith! When it looks as though everything we have will be taken from us—we may be stripped or put down or left out or ignored—yet we know God will judge the wicked. When people sneer at us or laugh—when the conniving ones get their way and the scheming ones seem to get ahead and the selfish ones seem to pile up all that they have—still we know that God will judge them. We know God will work these things out. And even if we should lose every single thing we have while we are here,

> Yet I will rejoice in the Lord, I will joy in the God of my salvation. The Lord God is my strength, and he will make my feet like hinds feet, and he will make me to walk upon mine high places (Hab. 3:18–19).

This is the triumphant assurance of the believer as revealed to Habakkuk. All of this came to his mind as he looked into the face of God.

And this can be your resort and mine. When it looks as though there is no way we can turn with any kind of assurance and confidence, we can look up. We should look into the presence of God and stand still; and God will speak into our hearts the words of His promise that will ground us and give us strength, confidence, and a triumphant sense of victory. Even though we may be stripped of all the things we might humanly want to have, we can rejoice in the God of our salvation.

Thus a marvelous note of triumph is to be found in this book. Habakkuk looked at the darkest hour and saw the saved star arise and the lights begin to shine from the very presence of God.

ZEPHANIAH

† † †

ZEPHANIAH WAS A preacher primarily to God's people. He had something to say to the world outside in chapter 2, but his major message was preached to the people of God. This book does not seem to focus on a specific problem, as Habakkuk does. But if we were to cite a single theme, it would be "the day of the Lord."

The prophets of those Old Testament times spoke of "the day of the Lord." The word "day" as it is used in the Hebrew has a variety of senses, much the same as it does in English. "Day" is not limited to a twenty-four-hour period. We can speak about how a certain person acted in the "day" of his youth; that might refer to six, seven, or eight years. When Scripture speaks of "the day of the Lord," it is used in the same way, namely, a period of time.

"The day of the Lord" contrasts with this day in which we are living. As Scripture speaks of "the day of the Lord," so it would call this time that we are living in "the day of man." What this means is that things happen today pretty much the way people want them to happen. Events seem to happen largely according to human nature. We know God overrules in providence, and to that extent He exercises a sort of veto power over events. A person may make plans, and if God

were to call him or her out of the world, that would be the end
of the person's plans.

But God apparently does not always interfere with people's
actions. This does not mean He is disinterested, and it does
not mean that He will never put His will into effect. Because
that is not true. The Bible seems to set before us the fact that
man was in a sense turned loose in this world. And he was
permitted, as it were, to go on with his affairs as far as this
world is concerned. It seems circumstances were put in his
hands. This is the kind of day in which we are living. We
could very well call this the day of man.

The Bible predicts a day when God will reveal Himself,
move out in front from behind the scenes, and will take
charge. The day of the Lord is a conception of the time when
God will move in and take over; it is not the case now. You
and I trust in God. Our faith enters beyond the veil. We
cannot see physically or always identify humanly what God is
doing now: the ways of God are past finding out. But there
will be a day when we "shall know as we are known." The
Lord Jesus said to His disciples, "What I do thou knowest not
now, but thou shalt know hereafter" (John 13:7). The Scriptures promise over and over again that there will be a day
when God will move and take over and establish His way
openly and manifestly. In that day certain things will happen.
Zephaniah preached that message.

Some of us will remember in our own spiritual experience
the time when we did pretty much as we pleased. We did not
get away with it, and we did not get to do all we wanted to do,
but we made our plans and we went whither we wanted to
go—at least we tried. Some of us will recall there came a day
when we yielded to the Lord. We turned ourselves over to
Him.

If your heart is like mine, you are wishing now under God
that He would take over completely as far as your life is concerned. Your common daily concern is "What does the Lord
want me to do?" Someone will ask you, "What are you going
to do next week? What are you going to do about this?" Some
will respond, not always openly, "I would like to have a little
time to pray about it." Such are people who want God to
begin His operation in them. In these cases, I am disposed to

think the day of the Lord has already begun internally in him. The Lord has already begun His operation in him.

I have no doubt that there will also be a time in which the day of the Lord will happen in outward affairs, in public events. People will carry on up to a certain point, and then the whole atmosphere will change and affairs will be taken over by a Power outside of humanity. Events will be brought to the conclusion and the completion that God has in mind. This would be the day of the Lord.

All through the Scriptures such truth is implied. In the parable of the master (Matt. 25), the good man went away from home and left talents to his servants—five to one, two to another, and one to another—to occupy until he would return. There will come a day when the Good Man will return and call all His servants to account. When that time for accounting comes, the sheep will go to His right hand and the goats to His left.

Zephaniah preached in his time, "Mark my words. Harvest will come just as surely as you live." Just now we may seem to be getting away with evil, but there will be a showdown. Payday is coming.

Men can do much evil in their time and may seem to be immune from any punishment; other men can do so much good in their time and may seem to be forsaken; but this is just a misunderstanding. We draw a wrong conclusion if we think that is the way it is going to be. God will act.

When God does move, and the day of the Lord begins, certain things will follow. All this was demonstrated in Israel's history. The day of the Lord did begin in Israel. There was a time when God did take over, and that is what Zephaniah was warning them about. Notice how Zephaniah's message is introduced:

> The word of the Lord which came unto Zephaniah the son of Cushi, the son of Gedaliah, the son of Amariah, the son of Hizkiah, in the days of Josiah the son of Amon, king of Judah (Zeph. 1:1).

It is generally thought that this indicates Zephaniah was one of the royal household, a member of the royal family. If that should be the case, he was one of the nobles and a man of high

family status. This would have made him very different from
the prophet Amos, who, we recall, was from the countryside.

> I will utterly consume all things from off the land, saith the
> Lord (Zeph. 1:2).

That was the way the message of Zephaniah began. Zephaniah
warned Israel that when God moved in, there would be
wholesale and widespread judgment.

> I will consume man and beast; I will consume the fowls of the
> heaven, and the fishes of the sea, and the stumbling blocks
> with the wicked; and I will cut off man from off the land, saith
> the Lord. I will also stretch out mine hand upon Judah . . .
> (Zeph. 1:3–4).

Zephaniah adds in verse 12, "I will search Jerusalem." Looking ahead into chapter 2, we see that "Gaza shall be forsaken,
and Ashkelon a desolation" (v. 4); Canaan, the land of the
Philistines, will be destroyed (v. 5); Moab shall be as Sodom,
and Ammon as Gomorrah (vv. 8–9); the Ethiopians will be
destroyed (v. 12); the Assyrians also (v. 13). Zephaniah
seemed to let his searchlight move all around; he took them
all in. When God moves, everyone will be brought to judgment.

> I will also stretch out mine hand upon Judah, and upon all the
> inhabitants of Jerusalem; and I will cut off the remnant of Baal
> from this place (Zeph. 1:4).

Baal worship had reached its highest peak in the days of Ahab,
king of Israel, and Athaliah, queen of Judah. But in the time of
Elisha, King Jehu rose up and killed off the Baal worshipers in
the north, and the priest Jehoiada led the insurrection that
killed Athaliah and eradicated the Baal worshipers in the
south. Baal worship never again became a prominent feature
of Israel's life.

But a remnant of naturalism continued.

> I will cut off the remnant of Baal from this place, and the name
> of the Chemarims with the priests; and them that worship the
> host of heaven upon the housetops; and them that worship and
> that swear by the Lord, and that swear by Malcham; and them
> that are turned back from the Lord; and those that have not
> sought the Lord, nor inquired for him (Zeph. 1:4–6).

Zephaniah prophesied that certain pagan deities would be wiped out. Some of the people of Israel had worshiped the sun, moon, and stars as the pagans did. But judgment was to come upon everyone: those who had fallen away from God, who used to walk with the Lord and now did not; and the people who had not come to God at all. Zephaniah said God would make a clean sweep.

The prophet warned Israel: "Hold thy peace at the presence of the Lord God" (1:7). They were to keep quiet now, for the day of the Lord was at hand. God would move, and the first thing God does when He moves is to call men in and have a settling up with them.

> . . . For the Lord hath prepared a sacrifice, he hath bid his guests. And it shall come to pass in the day of the Lord's sacrifice, that I will punish the princes, and the king's children, and all such as are clothed with strange apparel (Zeph. 1:7–8).

"With strange apparel" refers to people who were exceptionally well dressed. Their clothes had come from foreign countries. These people in Jerusalem would buy clothing that had been manufactured, we will say, in Babylon or Tyre or Sidon. Zephaniah was speaking of the rich.

> In the same day also will I punish all those that leap on the threshold, which fill their masters' houses with violence and deceit (Zeph. 1:9).

This verse seems to refer to some kind of pagan religious practice. This was probably some sort of exercise of worshiping natural gods. Apparently one of the things they did was to leap up and down at the thresholds of their homes to call the blessing of their gods upon them. These were another class of people who, like the rich, would be brought to judgment.

> And it shall come to pass in that day, saith the Lord, that there shall be the noise of a cry from the fish gate, and a howling from the second, and a great crashing from the hills. Howl, ye inhabitants of Maktesh, for all the merchant people are cut down; all they that bear silver are cut off. And it shall come to pass at that time, that I will search Jerusalem with candles . . . (Zeph. 1:10–12).

Zephaniah chooses this way to say that things were really going to be awful when the Lord came in to take over. God would put candles in all the dark places to see just how people were behaving. When God comes to judge there will be no hidden spots. He is going to open up everything.

> . . . And punish the men that are settled on their lees: that say in their heart, The Lord will not do good, neither will he do evil. Therefore their goods shall become a booty, and their houses a desolation: they shall also build houses, but not inhabit them; and they shall plant vineyards, but not drink the wine thereof (Zeph. 1:12–13).

These people were to be badly disappointed because they took it easy; they thought nothing was going to happen. But it did. When God moved, many of the things they counted on they would have no more.

> The great day of the Lord is near, it is near, and hasteth greatly, even the voice of the day of the Lord: the mighty man shall cry there bitterly. That day is a day of wrath, a day of trouble and distress, a day of wasteness and desolation, a day of darkness and gloominess, a day of clouds and thick darkness, a day of the trumpet and alarm against the fenced cities, and against the high towers. And I will bring distress upon men, that they shall walk like blind men, because they have sinned against the Lord: and their blood shall be poured out as dust, and their flesh as the dung. Neither their silver nor their gold shall be able to deliver them in the day of the Lord's wrath; but the whole land shall be devoured by the fire of his jealousy: for he shall make even a speedy riddance of all them that dwell in the land (Zeph. 1:14–18).

Zephaniah preached toward the end of the period of Judah's great glory and success. It was just before the coming of the Babylonians. He warned Judah of what was going to happen, and the people must have found him very unpleasant. He was a very unpopular preacher. But Zephaniah simply said God would act. God would judge. And when He judged, they would be in a bad way because they had not been walking in the way of the Lord.

In chapter 2 we come to the characteristic appeal of all the prophets.

> Gather yourselves together, yea, gather together, O nation not desired; before the decree bring forth, before the day pass as the chaff, before the fierce anger of the Lord come upon you, before the day of the Lord's anger come upon you. Seek ye the Lord . . . (Zeph. 2:1–3).

Woe unto the inhabitants of the sea coast, the nation of the Cherethites! the word of the Lord is against you; O Canaan, the land of the Philistines, I will even destroy thee, that there shall be no inhabitant (Zeph. 2:5).

In the houses of Ashkelon shall they lie down in the evening: for the Lord their God shall visit them, and turn away their captivity. I have heard the reproach of Moab, and the revilings of the children of Ammon, whereby they have reproached my people, and magnified themselves against their border (Zeph. 2:7–8).

God is saying, with reference to Moab and Ammon, "I have seen how they treated my people." Then He goes on to say:

Therefore as I live, saith the Lord of hosts, the God of Israel, Surely Moab shall be as Sodom, and the children of Ammon as Gomorrah, even the breeding of nettles, and saltpits, and a perpetual desolation: the residue of my people shall spoil them, and the remnant of my people shall possess them (Zeph. 2:9).

The very cities themselves will be so destroyed that they will be just like wasteland.

This shall they have for their pride, because they have reproached and magnified themselves against the people of the Lord of hosts. The Lord will be terrible unto them: for he will famish all the gods of the earth; and men shall worship him, every one from his place, even all the isles of the heathen. Ye Ethiopians also, ye shall be slain by my sword. And he will stretch out his hand against the north, and destroy Assyria; and will make Nineveh a desolation, and dry like a wilderness (Zeph. 2:10–13).

The prophet said that when God came to act, He would deal with other countries in addition to Israel and Judah. In other words, the day of the Lord will certainly begin with the day of judgment. Judgment will begin at the house of God, but it will go out to all people. And in chapter 3 Zephaniah's message continues much the same way. But in the latter part of the chapter, the curtain is lifted, and the day then begins to break. Chapter 3 begins, however, by saying:

Woe to her that is filthy and polluted, to the oppressing city! She obeyed not the voice; she received not correction; she trusted not in the Lord; she drew not near to her God (Zeph. 3:1–2).

What an indictment this was to the people of Israel. God sent
prophets to Jerusalem. He sent prophets to Judah. Thus God
told the people what to do. But "she obeyed not the voice":
Judah would not listen to the preaching. "She received not
correction": Judah would not take advice. "She trusted not in
the Lord": Judah went her own way. "She drew not near to
her God": Judah shunned the truth.

Some believers among us are inclined to obey the Lord in
that they turn their faces to the Lord Jesus Christ. They are
willing to receive correction to the extent that they would
confess their sins. They might even exercise true faith and
trust in the Lord. But is it not true that in many cases we fail
to draw near to God? God notices our hearts. If on any given
day we do not want to come close, if there is not in us some
initiative to draw nearer and nearer to God, then God sees
that in us. It is a mark of our failure, and He recognizes it. If
we are content with ourselves when we disobey the Lord, it is
not pleasing to Him. This is what Zephaniah pointed out with
reference to Judah.

> Therefore wait ye upon me, saith the Lord, until the day that I
> rise up to the prey: for my determination is to gather the
> nations, that I may assemble the kingdoms, to pour upon them
> mine indignation, even all my fierce anger: for all the earth
> shall be devoured with the fire of my jealousy. For then will I
> turn to the people a pure language, that they may all call upon
> the name of the Lord, to serve him with one consent (Zeph.
> 3:8–9).

The day of the Lord begins with judgment. God will deal with
all people in judgment. But when God has dealt with His
people in judgment, He will so affect them that in their hearts
they will call upon the name of the Lord with one voice. God
will affect His people in such a way that they will unite to
come near to Him.

> In that day shalt thou not be ashamed for all thy doings,
> wherein thou hast transgressed against me: for then I will take
> away out of the midst of thee them that rejoice in thy pride,
> and thou shalt no more be haughty because of my holy moun-
> tain. I will also leave in the midst of thee an afflicted and poor
> people, and they shall trust in the name of the Lord (Zeph.
> 3:11–12).

What a description this is of a believing heart—afflicted because of sin, poor in themselves, yet trusting in the name of the Lord!

> The remnant of Israel shall not do iniquity, nor speak lies;
> neither shall a deceitful tongue be found in their mouth: for
> they shall feed and lie down, and none shall make them afraid
> (Zeph. 3:13).

This is the day toward which we are moving—when God begins to act.

> Sing, O daughter of Zion; shout, O Israel; be glad and rejoice
> with all the heart, O daughter of Jerusalem (Zeph. 3:14).

Zephaniah told how God would take away the people's judgments. He would cast out the enemy.

> The Lord thy God in the midst of thee is mighty; he will save,
> he will rejoice over thee with joy; he will rest in his love, he
> will joy over thee with singing (Zeph. 3:17).

> At that time will I bring you again, even in the time that I
> gather you: for I will make you a name and a praise among all
> people of the earth, when I turn back your captivity before
> your eyes, saith the Lord (Zeph. 3:20).

Thus ends the message of Zephaniah, the evangelist and revivalist of God. There is a bright day coming by and by. There will be glory when God reveals Himself. The great day of the Lord will begin with judgment; and in that judgment He will destroy the wicked. The chaff will be burned with fire, but the wheat He will gather into the granary, and He will keep it. And in that day when God's will is done, all the strain and the stress will be gone; and things will be as they ought to be. Singing and rejoicing and shouting and gladness of heart will prevail.

HAGGAI

† † †

HAGGAI IS A short book, and like other short books, it focuses on one main idea. Haggai is centered in one event. The
message is a success story in the midst of failure. God's people
were in a situation where their program had "bogged down."
Something they had undertaken to do in the name of the Lord
had come to ground. They were not getting ahead with it.
And they were not happy. They were not blessed. They did
not see how they could go on with the task.

Haggai started to preach about the building of the second
temple. Back in earlier history, Moses had led the children of
Israel out of the land of Egypt. They constituted themselves a
nation in the wilderness and afterward in the Promised Land.
The pattern and design of their fellowship was to have a tabernacle in the center of their encampment, which was to be
the dwelling place of God. God would thereby be demon-
strating and typifying a great truth: He would be in the midst
of His people.

This truth is variously stated in the Bible, generally with
words like this: "And [I] will be a Father unto you, and ye
shall be my sons and daughters, saith the Lord Almighty"
(2 Cor. 6:18). Or like this: "I will be their God, and they shall
be my people" (2 Cor. 6:16). This phrase occurs over and over

in both the Old Testment and in the New. This was the significance of the second name given to Jesus when He was born: Emmanuel, "God with us."

The very essence of the Gospel is "God with us." The vital element in the truth in Christ is God will be with us, and we will be with God. But there must be a basic, intimate, personal, vital fellowship, communion, and oneness between the soul and God. The best analogy to this on earth is when husband and wife come together to become one flesh. Sometimes the illustration is used of a branch and a vine: so close that life goes through both and bears fruit. The very essence of the Gospel is that the human soul and the living God are to be united, are to be in harmony. In this union, the believing soul is to be blessed with peace and joy and strength and fruitfulness.

Now, in the New Testament there are special words to express this idea. This is the Holy Spirit dwelling in us. The Gospel tells of the Son of God coming into the world to call us to God and to reconcile us to Him, to make effectual the atonement. The word "atonement" comes from the verb "atone," and the verb "atone" suggests the phrase "at one." And this conveys the reason why Jesus of Nazareth died: He wanted to "atone" us with God, to bring us together with God.

When the children of Israel came out of the land of Egypt and began to live as a nation on their own, they were arranged at their encampments in the desert in a definite pattern. Three tribes were to be to the north of the tabernacle, three tribes to the east, three tribes to the south, and three to the west. In the tabernacle, in the holy place, even closer in the holy of holies—in the very center was the mercy seat. At the mercy seat God would meet with His people face to face, symbolizing the very center of their lives.

Later on, with the passing of the tabernacle, the temple was built by Solomon. The temple was arranged, like the tabernacle, so that God would be symbolically in the very center of the people. All the people were related to God. But God is related to all the people like the hub of a wheel, like the trunk of a tree, with everything coming out from Him.

The first temple was destroyed by the Babylonians when

they took the Jews captive and led them away. After the Jews returned to the land they were to rebuild the temple. In this way they would reestablish the symbolic dwelling place of God in their midst. They had started on the project, but when it was half completed, they stopped.

There is probably nothing more pathetic than a half-finished structure. The people began construction on a pretentious scale, with all good will, enthusiasm, and inspiration. But there was not enough money to finish it. And so they did not finish it. Thus there was a half-finished temple in Jerusalem when Haggai began preaching.

> Thus speaketh the Lord of hosts, saying, This people say, The time is not come, the time that the Lord's house should be built (Hag. 1:2).

Have you ever heard such an excuse? "It is not the right time. What is wrong with this program is that we did not begin at the right time. . . . We should have started two years ago. . . . We should have waited until we had this new development out here. If we had just waited long enough we would have finished it by now. . . . It is not a good time now because summer is coming on, and that is a poor time to start anything. We should wait until next fall. . . . But it is not a good thing to start in the fall, because Thanksgiving is coming up and then Christmas. You know how it is at Christmas time—nobody ever does anything. . . . Anyway, it is not a good thing to start anything in January because by that time everyone is looking forward to April 15 and they have those taxes to pay, and you know what that is like" . . . and on and on.

There never is time for people who cannot find the right time. The Jews at the time of Haggai said, "It is not the time to build the house of the Lord." Then Haggai started preaching.

> Is it time for you, O ye, to dwell in your ceiled houses, and this house lie waste? (Hag. 1:4).

The people probably had houses that were finished with pinewood—lovely woodwork for their homes. To have a ceiling roofed in with wood like that in those days was really high class. People had the most modern houses of the day, but the place of worship was really in a poor state. So the preacher Haggai challenged them: "Is it time for you to have your fine dwellings, when you are not building the house of the Lord?"

> Now therefore thus saith the Lord of hosts; Consider your ways. Ye have sown much, and bring in little; ye eat, but ye have not enough; ye drink, but ye are not filled with drink; ye clothe you, but there is none warm; and he that earneth wages earneth wages to put it into a bag with holes (Hag. 1:5–6).

We are not being blessed. We work and we have nothing to show for it. We struggle and we are not satisfied. With all the effort we are putting out, we never achieve happiness. Haggai tells us why: "You have not been working at the things God wants you to do."

> Ye looked for much, and, low, it came to little; and when ye brought it home, I did blow upon it. Why? saith the Lord of hosts. Because of mine house that is waste, and ye run every man unto his own house (Hag. 1:9).

The people worked and worked for something, and when they got the little bit and were going to take it home, the Lord just blew it away. So they had nothing. All the time they were looking to their own things, and they did not pay attention to the things of the Lord, so there was no blessing on them. That was the preacher's message.

Haggai is considered a great preacher, so I expect that the people listened to him. Haggai went on to declare the word of the Lord in these words:

> Therefore the heaven over you is stayed from dew, and the earth is stayed from her fruit. And I called for a drought upon the land, and upon the mountains, and upon the corn, and upon the new wine, and upon the oil, and upon that which the ground bringeth forth, and upon men, and upon cattle, and upon all the labor of the hands (Hag. 1:10–11).

God would let nothing prosper for them.

> Then Zerubbabel the son of Shealtiel, and Joshua the son of Josedech, the high priest, with all the remnant of the people, obeyed the voice of the Lord their God, and the words of Haggai the prophet, as the Lord their God had sent him, and the people did fear before the Lord. Then spake Haggai the Lord's messenger in the Lord's message unto the people, saying, I am with you, saith the Lord (Hag. 1:12–13).

When the leaders and the people obeyed the voice of the Lord, He assured them of the blessing of His presence.

> And the Lord stirred up the spirit of Zerubbabel the son of Shealtiel, governor of Judah, and the spirit of Joshua the son of Josedech, the high priest, and the spirit of all the remnant of the people; and they came and did work in the house of the Lord of hosts, their God (Hag. 1:14).

When people responded to preaching like that, things picked right up and went along wonderfully.

> Speak now to Zerubbabel the son of Shealtiel, governor of Judah, and to Joshua the son of Josedech, the high priest, and to the residue of the people, saying, Who is left among you that saw this house in her first glory? and how do ye see it now? is it not in your eyes in comparison of it as nothing? (Hag. 2:2–3).

The old-timers who had seen the temple of Solomon could see that this new construction could not compare with it.

> Yet now be strong, O Zerubbabel, saith the Lord; and be strong, O Joshua, son of Josedech, the high priest; and be strong, all ye people of the land, saith the Lord, and work: for I am with you, saith the Lord of hosts (Hag. 2:4).

Be strong and work, Haggai was saying. What the people were building was not as pretentious as the former temple, but they were to work at it.

> According to the word that I covenanted with you when ye came out of Egypt, so my spirit remaineth among you: fear ye not. For thus saith the Lord of hosts; Yet once, it is a little while, and I will shake the heavens, and the earth, and the sea, and the dry land; and I will shake all nations, and the desire of all nations shall come: and I will fill this house with glory, saith the Lord of hosts (Hag. 2:5–7).

Even though the second temple was not as big or pretentious as the first, God would be with them and He would fill this house with glory.

> The silver is mine, and the gold is mine, saith the Lord of hosts. The glory of this latter house shall be greater than of the former, saith the Lord of hosts: and in this place will I give peace, saith the Lord of hosts (Hag. 2:8–9).

Here is a marvelous prophecy.

The phrase "desire of all nations" refers to the coming of the

Messiah, the Lord Jesus Christ. This much can be said historically: the Lord Jesus stood in that second temple. He never stood physically in the first one. The first temple of Solomon was a great and pretentious building, the like of which was never built again. The second temple was small and meager by comparison, but God was telling the people through Haggai that this one would be more blessed than the former. The glory of the latter house would be greater than that of the former, because the Prince of Peace Himself would stand in this one.

People today could preach this message for the finishing of a sanctuary they are building for their congregation, raising the money, and paying up their pledges. It would be all right if a new building were needed, but let us not miss the main thought of Haggai's message. Believers today face something more profound and more personal than the construction of a church building. There is an important truth we need to keep in mind. Churches are not made of stone or brick. In the last analysis it is not the church building that counts. It is not the church building that is the temple of the Lord.

The believer in Christ is the temple of the Lord. It is the spirit in the believer that is the temple of the Lord. We can say that the first temple for the believer exists when he first receives Jesus Christ consciously as his Savior. Some believers are brought up in the truth of the Gospel and probably never really know life apart from the Gospel. Some believers receive Christ as adults, and they are very conscious of what happened at the time.

It is possible that in the glory of our conversion, in the euphoria of our first turning to God, we want to be something special in His sight. We may believe we will do something important in His sight. As new believers we intend to be "real Christians." It may be we believe we will become a Sunday school teacher and win many people into the church. Perhaps we believe that if others will ever let us be president of the women of the church, we will really produce a good program.

It is possible that we all have big dreams and great intentions when we start in our Christian experience. When we take Jesus Christ as our Savior and know we are really destined for heaven, we have a wonderful sense of joy and peace, and we look to become a zealous, strong believer. We may even plan to read the Bible regularly and to pray regularly. We plan to attend church regularly and expect to do many things in the way of service. We expect to be strong in faith and experience and receive God's blessing. Nothing will ever go wrong.

There are people who started out strong in living as believers in Christ who have been inwardly devastated by their own frustrations and defeat. They have tried, but their efforts have not succeeded. The enemy has come in and destroyed everything they had. Their names may be still on the church roll, but they no longer have hopes of regular prayer. They no longer have any promises that they can believe for themselves. They no longer plan to read the Bible regularly because they know better than that: they know they are not going to do it. What has happened is that the temple in the heart has been broken down, so the Lord is not living there. They may believe He is in heaven, and they may trust Him to save them, but they walk alone.

People like these will come Sunday morning to church. They scarcely dare to listen to a good sermon for fear they will get their hopes up in vain—because it is not going to be good on Monday, Tuesday, Wednesday, Thursday, or Friday. Finally some of them stop coming to church at all. They are not happy.

Do not for a moment believe that I do not feel in my heart a great hunger and compassion for them. I am simply recognizing realistically that this is the way it is. Do you know what such people need? They need to come out of their captivity. They need to come out of Babylon. They need to come away from the bondage of the world. They need to come back to the land, back to the city of God, back to fellowship with Him.

Some of us may have had such experience when it dawned on us we might never be anyone great; we might not be nearly so big as we said we were going to be. But we could still have genuine fellowship with the Lord. We were ready to rebuild the temple in our hearts. It would not be as big or as glorious a temple as in the day of our conversion. The pretentiousness of consecration is never as great as that of conversion. When a person is a new believer it is so easy to think everything will be wonderful. When a person is more experienced and has experienced suffering and defeat, he has learned to distrust himself. He does not believe in himself any more. His realtionship with God is on a very humble basis.

And so this person can have a more glorious experience than ever before. His temple will never seem as pretentious. He will never be as full of himself as he had been, but he can have the Prince Himself in his soul. Such a person needs to let his heart be the temple of the Lord Jesus Christ. He needs to let the reality of the Holy Spirit in him be genuine. He needs to realize that the Lord stands at the door and knocks. If he will open, the Lord will come in and dine with him. "Abide in me and I in you": these words of Jesus to His disciples point to the dwelling place of the Lord. "Abide in me and I in you": Christ will dwell in our hearts by faith.

The message of Haggai is the message of a believer in Christ, a true child of God, who has somehow drifted into a state of barren futility, with all good intentions half-done, with things started that got nowhere. Such a person can start in again where he is. He can build more humbly. He need not make any promises to himself about reading the Bible through every few months. He would be wise to start with little things: he could read *some* in the Bible. Perhaps he cannot pray for everyone; perhaps he does not know how to pray, but he can pray *some*. He should begin with simple things. He should try to understand the promises of God about living in Him. He should devote himself to understanding how the Lord God Himself can be in his heart Monday, Tuesday, Wednesday, Thursday, Friday, and Saturday—in his home, and in his office. He should believe His presence.

God will forgive him. God will cleanse him. He will keep him. So he is never going to be much—what difference does that make? God will fill him. This believer will realize he is not nearly as great a servant as he thought he would be. But now that he knows what he is doing—and in this sense is more mature—and now that he really wants to fix things up for Christ to dwell in his heart, he will have greater glory in this humility than he ever had at the beginning. He can have greater glory.

It is common to talk about how wonderful the faith of little children is. And it *is* wonderful. But remember that children still do not know much. I appreciate what some people have in mind when they get the little ones to pray, because they pray so earnestly and sincerely. I do not discount that. But I also realize that children have not been hurt badly. When a person has been in sorrow, or someone faces something that disrupts his life, such as his health or a business failure, and it dawns on him that he is never going to amount to much or very far—when that person comes to know that God will come and dwell in his humble self, there will be a joy and a glory that no child ever knew. It will be the joy and the glory of a person who understands in a special way the wonderful grace of God. God comes to him, such as he is, ready to take him to Himself.

The life of a mature believer may be expressed in a very humble sigh. The little temple that he has now built in which he is going to fellowship with his Lord may be meager. But it can be filled with the very glory of God if he but lets God come in and dwell with him. That is the truth that was shown to Haggai.

The prophet told the people that God was calling to them: "Go out and look at it, and compare this second temple with the first temple. It is not nearly as large, not nearly as pretentious, but it will be more glorious. Because this second temple will be really the one in which the Prince of Peace Himself will stand." There will be peace in this second temple.

I am impressed with the truth to realize the glory that God offers to any sincere, humble, and mature Christian who will simply say, "Come, Lord Jesus. Come into my heart and live with me." This was the message of Haggai.

Haggai preached in such a way that his people did fear the Lord and reverently worshiped Him. In preparing this study of Haggai I received a great blessing personally. I realized I do not have to wait until I am perfect. I do not have to wait until I get to be an important person. The Lord wants to be with me as I am. And if I will just receive Him afresh and make Him a dwelling place, He will do everything. I do not have to turn on any lights—He brings the light. I will not have to worry about heating His room—Christ will warm it. I will not have to worry about furniture—Christ will furnish the whole thing. He will bring His wealth with Him.

Jesus wants to come and live with me. He will bring the glory of my considered, sober, deliberate, personal fellowship with the Lord. My body will be the temple of God, and peace will be there. This is what Haggai promised. And this is what the Jews received. May we also receive it.

ZECHARIAH

† † †

The Lord hath been sore displeased with your fathers. Therefore say thou unto them, Thus saith the Lord of hosts; Turn ye
unto me, saith the Lord of hosts, and I will turn unto you, saith
the Lord of hosts. Be ye not as your fathers, unto whom the
former prophets have cried, saying, Thus saith the Lord of
hosts; Turn ye now from your evil ways, and from your evil
doings: but they did not hear, nor hearken unto me, saith the
Lord. Your fathers, where are they? and the prophets, do they
live for ever? But my words and my statutes, which I com-
manded my servants the prophets, did they not take hold of
your fathers? and they returned and said, Like as the Lord of
hosts thought to do unto us, according to our ways, and according to our doings, so hath he dealt with us (Zech. 1:2-6).

THE MESSAGE OF Zechariah is a call for some of us to
break with some of our old traditions and move up a little
closer to God.

Zechariah urged the people of Israel not to act the way the
former generation did. God called them, and they did not
come. They found out that God judged just as He said He
would. So Zechariah urged his people to act a different way.

It is easy for churches to get to a point where they settle for
second best. This happens when they cannot get everyone to
agree on goals and plans for the future. One thing just about
everybody will agree on in a congregation is to sit still. Sitting

still does not require much argument. There may be a few people who keep stirring things up, but if the majority pay no attention to them and ignore them often enough, eventually they will become quiet. Then the congregation will all be at peace. All can go comfortably to sleep. This happens far too often with churches or even families who get to the place where they settle for something less than what is good enough.

This situation can happen also with individual believers in Christ. They settle down to a way of living that is not good enough. The Jews had intended life to be all it could be, but they stopped short—and then settled down. Zechariah pointed out that the Lord had been very displeased with their fathers. God did not like the way they ceased from their struggles. They stopped short. So the prophet had something to tell the next generation.

Zechariah records a number of visions, one after another. As we read them we will see many things we will not understand, but it will still be profitable to read them carefully.

Visions are to be handled like parables. A parable is a made-up story that represents real life. When a writer or speaker wants to illustrate a certain truth, he tells a story that he has made up. But the story must be such that the audience will say, "That could happen. That is the way it would happen." For example, a man goes out sowing seed, scattering it everywhere. The seeds fall into different kinds of ground. The good ground brings forth fruit, while the poor ground does not. Our reaction is, "This event could happen just like that." Or a fisherman throws a net into the sea and brings in fish. Some are good fish and some are bad. It really could happen that way. Again, a man goes out and sows wheat in his field. An enemy comes and sows weeds, so there will be wheat and weeds growing up in the same field. All that could be true: everyone who has had a garden knows it is true.

Parables are stories made up of earthly events that happen in such a way that they are believable by everyone. They are put together so as to be a story with a point to it that illustrates a truth. The story told to illustrate this truth is a parable.

Visions, on the other hand, are like dreams. A vision is like a dream in the way in which it would come to one of us. We do not feel we are responsible for the way it unfolds. Now, a parable teller—a storyteller—makes up the story. But the person who has a dream or a vision does not make it up. It comes to him.

It has been noted in the study of dreams that every single part in a dream is something that has been seen at one time or another. But the combination, we should note, may be something nobody has ever seen. In dreams a person is not troubled because of novelty. In the case of God's dealing with a man's soul—when He has brought something up out of the man's own experience, which the man feels is possible—He may bring His message to the dreamer in a way that the man feels could be true, even if he cannot understand the meaning. The things inside the man do not straighten out, and they do not make rhyme or reason in the things he feels. Such a man can have a vision. In a vision an idea shines into the heart, where it fits and brings all parts together into a real thing.

A vision is like the missing piece in a jigsaw puzzle. In his whole heart, in all his consciousness, the person has all the parts of this jigsaw puzzle, but without this missing piece it does not make sense. Then in the vision something flashes, and when that piece is in there, the man in his heart makes sense. But if someone else hears the account of the vision, yet does not have the other parts of the jigsaw puzzle in his heart, what he has heard about the vision is just an extra piece of jigsaw puzzle—it will not make any sense.

Something like this happens when some people read the Bible. Or in listening to preaching. A preacher needs to realize that as he is preaching, some people sitting before him have the other parts of the puzzle in their hearts already. The minister may preach the right word that fits in the consciousness. There may be much truth in the heart of the hearer about which the preacher may not even know. This is the way it is with much Bible teaching. If someone reads a portion of the Bible and says, "I read it all right, but I could not make heads or tails of it," it is because that person does not have the other parts in his heart. So the message is not operative in him. Some people in Bible times heard the Lord Jesus tell parables, but they did not know what the stories meant.

Today people can read these visions of Zechariah and not

know what they mean. But when a person's heart is prepared, the visions fit. The Holy Spirit brings truth to people by this means. In a vision the picture illustrates the idea, and the interpretation points to the meaning. Like a dream as far as its parts are concerned, a vision is often incoherent; it may seem chaotic. But it leaves a definite impression. When the heart is full of the facts involved, and the mind cannot see the relationship or the meaning of those facts, then a vision flashes the pattern of truth into the mind that will be grasped by such as are ready. "He that hath ears to hear, let him hear"! This is what Jesus of Nazareth said at times when He was interpreting parables or visions (see Matt. 11:15; 13:9, 43 for example).

Have you ever thought about that Scripture? "He that hath ears to hear, let him hear." Do we know what it means to have an ear to hear? It is to have a heart that is ready. Now, unless the person's heart is ready, he will never guess what the Scripture is saying. Much that Jesus of Nazareth said will go by the board with people who have not been prepared for those words.

When we are interpreting parables, we must not force details out of them. For instance, the parable of the ten virgins at a wedding (Matt. 25), with five wise and five foolish, is a simple story with a simple message: the Lord is coming back. Some virgins thought the bridegroom might come back at any time and had oil on hand for their lamps; some were not thoughtful of His return, so they did not have oil with them. The point is that the believer should be ready for Jesus' return. That is all that means. Some might ask, "Who are the five wise, and who are the five foolish?" Then they might hunt either in Scripture or in their experiences and try to name them, saying, "These are the foolish virgins over there, and these are the five wise virgins here."

This would be faulty interpretation. If people stay with what the parable is about—namely the Lord may return at any time and we must be ready—they would arrive at the truth. They would understand that the Lord is likely to come back at any time. They would say to themselves, "I ought to be ready." That is the reason for the parable. All attempts at further interpretation garble the matter so that one can miss the whole point. The same holds true with visions.

Sometimes true believers fall out with each other so they cannot even be friendly because they think that the red horse in Revelation means this and the pale horse means that, whereas the other person says, "No, the red horse means that, and the pale horse means this." Sometimes someone will ask about the Antichrist: who is he? Through the years many different persons have been supposed to be "the Antichrist." Guessing names is a quick way to start trouble in a church and to make bad friends out of good people. Rather than trying to identify the elements of visions, or identifying the elements of parables, why not let the truth bear in on us? If we will let the truth bear in on us, God will do more.

So let us not force any kind of details into a parable or into a vision. Let Scripture speak to us, and we will be blessed as we read the fascinating portions of Scripture.

It is worth noting that four books in the Bible are particularly full of visions. It happens that each one of them was written at a time when God's people were governed by hostile, alien forces. The four visionary books are two "major prophets," Ezekiel and Daniel, and this "minor prophet," Zechariah, and then the Book of Revelation. Ezekiel was a captive at the river Chebar in Babylonia. Daniel was a captive in the city of Babylon. In the days of Zechariah, the Jews had been captives in Persia and were returning to Judah under foreign mandate. At the time the Book of Revelation was written, John was an exile on the isle of Patmos. Every one of these men was a prisoner to some extent. Every one of these men ministered to his people under the auspices, you might say, of a foreign power. It has been suggested that at times when the governing power was unsympathetic, the prophet would speak in visions. When the authorities heard the message, they would not know what the prophet was talking about; but the believers would know.

A missionary to Japan, a Mr. Talmadge, was captured, arrested by the Japanese authorities, and thrown into a concentration camp during World War II. For some time he was not allowed to have any kind of printed materials. Finally they permitted him to have one book. Astonishingly, the one book he asked for was a Hebrew Bible. Talmadge did this because he thought he would keep busy studying it. He had had some

Hebrew in seminary, but it had not affected him much, so he wanted now to study it; this would give him something to do in prison. A copy of the Hebrew Bible was given to him, and he began to read it and study the Hebrew. Remembering the English translation pretty well, he could figure out most words. He sought to understand the construction and the grammar of the language.

The Japanese became very suspicious of this Hebrew Bible because they felt it probably was a code by which some military instructions were included. So they took this Book to have their experts break the code and find out the military information behind it. They worked on it and worked on it, and eventually they brought the Book back to him and asked him to translate it. This he did. He opened the Book and read, "In the beginning God created the heavens and the earth. And the earth was without form, and void," and so on. But the Japanese decided Talmadge was just putting on an act. So they listened to him and made notes of what he said, but they did not believe him. Then they took the Book again and kept it for a long time. They worked with all the experts, but they never could figure out what the code was.

There are some people who are just about the same way with the English Bible as the Japanese military were with the Hebrew text. They come to it with a heart and spirit that are not in keeping with its purpose. Sometimes their interest is not really the interest of the Lord. Perhaps they want only to prove a point. Perhaps they want only to master something. We can miss the truth if we approach something in the wrong way. We will not get the truth of a matter by mastering it; it must master us.

What will happen if we let something master us? What will the Bible do to us if we let it master us? The Bible will show us not only the emptiness of ourselves and the riches of the grace of the Lord Jesus Christ, but also most of all the love of God toward us. And the Bible will call us out to commit ourselves in love toward Him and in love toward everyone else. All the interpretation that we may have that does not bear truthfully on that theme we will find dry in our hands. We will tend to waste our time and our spirit; but if we will humbly come to the Scriptures and let them speak to our hearts, they will draw us closer and closer to personal fellowship with the living Lord Jesus Christ and bring Him closer and closer to us until the great purpose of God's Word is accomplished so that we have communion with God. Such a person will serve God and will serve others in the name of the Lord to the glory of God.

MALACHI

† † †

THE NAME "MALACHI" is actually a phrase meaning "My servant." It is a common opinion among Bible students that the name "Malachi" may not have been the name of any one man. The man who actually did the preaching in this book may have had some other name. In his function he was "My servant"—God's messenger.

It is strikingly fitting that this should be the last book in the Old Testament and the last in the series of the prophets. There are the Major Prophets and the Minor Prophets, and here in Malachi is a man who seems to gather the whole message together and present the issue clearly before us. It seems fitting that he should have the title "My servant."

There is something significant in the last prophet. There being no more prophets does not mean that God is finished, but it brings to our minds that time has run out. In Israel's history, God's work had run its time. It was like the cutting of a crop of wheat. The wheat grows all summer long, but when the harvest time comes and when the reaper goes through, that is the end of the crop of wheat. There may be another crop in the future, but this crop is over. So it was with Judah.

God had warned Judah and pleaded with the people. He told them that if they did not turn to Him, He would have to judge them and destroy them. It is true that in their case He would keep a remnant for Himself and eventually restore the people. But devastating ruin would come upon the nation—and it did. By the time Malachi came on the scene, Jerusalem had been destroyed. The temple had been destroyed. The people had been carried away and kept captive for seventy years. A whole generation had died in captivity, and the nation was blacked out. Through Malachi God sought to give His people a sense of the seriousness and the significance of living with Him.

No one can afford to let things go along indefinitely in an incomplete and unsettled fashion. A person must come to grips with God and do something about his life. When we speak about the last prophet, we get the feeling that there comes a time when we must say, "This is it. This is the show-down." We can call these the last words. The ninth inning is here. Things are going to be settled now. When this is past, everything will be all over. In this way Malachi is very significant.

Malachi was the last of the prophets, and in a real sense he was the representative of all the prophets, standing before the people who knew God, but who had not been faithful to God, and telling them, "It is later than you think."

This Book of Malachi reflects a normal development. As the season draws to its harvest, a certain ripening takes place. When the time of the harvest in human living draws near, people begin to show themselves in their true colors. The truth begins to appear in the fruit, in the way people live, in the way they think. Now we find that when God comes in judgment, that judgment begins at the house of God. In this world's experience, among God's people, there is a strain of carnality. There can be the negative expression of human nature among the very best people.

In our churches there can be this element of human nature to such an extent that many things we undertake will not come to pass. We are uncrucified. We have not really yielded ourselves entirely to God. How many times does a pastor sit down with his elders, or the board of deacons, or stewards and vestrymen, seeking to do the work of the church, and find among these people—the best men in his church—that some will not even talk to one another? What that does to the Lord's work only God Himself knows.

When God comes to judge—as come to judge He will—judgment will begin at the house of God. God will start with the preacher. He will begin with the most responsible person, and that person will be judged. Every other person down the line in that church will be judged, before God ever gets to judging the people in the community outside the church who are living wanton lives in riot and excess. God will first go through the churches in His judgment. He will judge the people who know better. God will judge the people who know that they should be praying, but do not. God will judge those who know they should be studying the Word of God, but do not. God will judge those who know they should be inviting people to church, but are not.

Malachi makes it clear that this is the way God will move. This does not justify the unbelievers, but it puts the responsibility where it belongs. It is quite true that a man who is blind is in a bad state, and a person who is lame will certainly limp; but it is the man who can see who has responsibility, and it is the man who is well who has the responsibility.

Malachi, representing all the prophets in the showdown period that signifies the coming of the end, comes bluntly forward and points his finger right at the believers themselves. He brings out that the evil in men's hearts, even among people who claim to know God, will show up at the time of the harvest. Malachi shows that evil in the heart of the believer shows up in a certain kind of insolence toward God. It is almost impudence.

This insolence is mentioned by Malachi over and over again.

> The burden of the word of the Lord to Israel by Malachi. I have loved you, saith the Lord. Yet ye say, Wherein hast thou loved us? Was not Esau Jacob's brother? saith the Lord: yet I loved Jacob (Mal. 1:1–2).

The words Malachi attributes to the people are backtalk, insolence, impudence. The Jews would say, "I do not see that this applies to me. I do not see that I come under this judgment. Even though the Word of God says, 'I have loved you,' I do not see that it makes much difference." In this the Jews

showed their ignorance of God's statement, as Malachi
pointed out, "I hated Esau, and I loved you." Malachi reported God as saying, "All through history I have never per-
petuated the flesh; I have kept you folks; but you have not
appreciated it." And the message continues,

> And your eyes shall see, and ye shall say, The Lord will be
> magnified from the border of Israel (Mal. 1:5).

Malachi goes on:

> A son honoreth his father, and a servant his master: if then I be
> a father, where is mine honor? and if I be a master, where is my
> fear? saith the Lord of hosts unto you, O priests, that despise
> my name. And ye say, Wherein have we despised thy name?
> (Mal. 1:6).

When the prophet would speak thus to the people and bring
to their minds that they had despised God, they would ask,
"How did we do that?" Malachi reported that God told them,
"Ye offer polluted bread upon mine altar" (v. 7). The sacrifices
they brought were unclean, and yet they asked, "Wherein
have we polluted thee?" God told them, "In that ye say, The
table of the Lord is contemptible." They said in effect that it
does not amount to much.

> And if ye offer the blind for sacrifice, is it not evil? (Mal. 1:8).

The people were supposed to bring in a lamb, a kid, or a goat
for sacrifice. Some of the creatures sold in the marketplace
would be better than others. When the people had a
blemished animal, such as a crippled one, they would bring it
and give it to the Lord. But the good ones they would sell on
the market.

    In how many cases is our charity to the poor a matter of
giving them the clothes we cannot wear? This is what the Jews
were doing. They went through the routine: they offered
sacrifices. But if a man had eight or nine sheep and one of
them was crippled and would not bring as much on the market, that is the one he would bring for sacrifice. God said, "I
see that. Do you think you are honoring me?"

    How many times have we been in a church and when the
matter of giving came up, we figured out how much we had
"left over," so that we could give painlessly? Then we would

add a little to that, and so we would give something. This is
the way it was with the Jews. And Malachi reminded them
that God saw everything they did.

When we bring some little thing to God, we are making
God little. What do we spend in a week? And what do we give
in a week? If Malachi were our preacher, he would tell us that
according to how we handle our finances we can see whether
we are honoring God. And when a church is spending more
money on amusement than on foreign missions, God does not
overlook that. Malachi told them God would deal with them
about this. They made God little, and God knew it. When
they asked, "How did we make God little?" Malachi told
them, "By the way you are giving to Him."

> But ye have profaned it, in that ye say, The table of the Lord is
> polluted; and the fruit thereof, even his meat, is contemptible.
> Ye said also, Behold, what a weariness is it! and ye have snuffed
> at it, saith the Lord of hosts; and ye brought that which was
> torn, and the lame, and the sick; thus ye brought an offering:
> should I accept this of your hand? saith the Lord. But cursed be
> the deceiver, which hath in his flock a male, and voweth, and
> sacrificeth unto the Lord a corrupt thing: for I am a great King,
> saith the Lord of hosts, and my name is dreadful among the
> heathen (Mal. 1:12–14).

God is entitled to something else than their second best. That
is Malachi's emphasis here.

> And now, O ye priests, this commandment is for you. If ye will
> not hear, and if ye will not lay it to heart, to give glory unto my
> name, saith the Lord of hosts, I will even send a curse upon
> you, and I will curse your blessings: yea, I will have cursed
> them already, because ye do not lay it to heart. Behold, I will
> corrupt your seed, and spread dung upon your faces, even the
> dung of your solemn feasts; and one shall take you away with it.
> And ye shall know that I have sent this commandment unto
> you, that my covenant might be with Levi, saith the Lord of
> hosts (Mal. 2:1–4).

Then Malachi went on and told the people positively what
God really wanted from them.

> My covenant was with him of life and peace; and I gave them to
> him for the fear wherewith he feared me, and was afraid before
> my name (Mal. 2:5).

God gave Levi life and peace because he feared, esteemed, and reverenced Him. Levi looked upon God as high and holy and lifted up, and he bowed himself down before God. Levi was a true priest. He adequately and wholly honored God. With Levi, nothing was too good for God: God came first.

This reminds us of a certain woman of Bethany. When she came to anoint the Lord, she brought a box of ointment that was very precious. It was the best she had. She poured it on Him. She was criticized by others who said that was an awful waste of money. She could have given it to the poor. But the Lord said, "Leave her alone. She has wrought a good work. She has done this thing for me" (Mark 14:6). All this is a way of saying that when a person comes to the Lord, he should bring the best he has. Then he will have done what he could to honor God. That is what God looks for. The Jews had not done this in Malachi's time.

> The law of truth was in his mouth, and iniquity was not found in his lips: he walked with me in peace and equity, and did turn many away from iniquity (Mal. 2:6).

What a picture this is of a true pastor, a true minister, a man who in faithfulness and sincerity walks with God, with the result that many people are turned to God by his ministry!

> For the priest's lips should keep knowledge, and they should seek the law at his mouth: for he is the messenger of the Lord of hosts (Mal. 2:7).

The knowledge that the priest's lips should keep is not a series of academic facts. The priest's lips should recognize God. The priest should have a sense of the proper esteem of God. The priest should talk in a way that honors God for what He is. If the minister, the church officer, or the active church member will honor God for what He is, there will be blessing on the people. Everyone else will be blessed.

Malachi 2:14 follows in this same vein of thought: "Yet ye say, Wherefore?" This is more of the same insolent backtalk. The people were saying, "Why should you blame us for the things that have happened? You accuse us of doing wrong; where have we done anything wrong?"

> . . . Because the Lord hath been witness between thee and the
> wife of thy youth, against whom thou hast dealt treacherously
> (Mal. 2:14).

These words deal with the heart's affection. They use the figure of the attachment between husband and wife to point up the attachment between the believer and God. The relationship between the believer's heart and God in heaven should be as close as the relationship between husband and wife. This is to say, they belong to each other.

This concept is not nearly so idealistic as it sounds. It is practical. No matter how unsatisfactory the husband may be, the wife will still not let anyone else come between them. She still belongs to him. He still belongs to her. As long as it is like that, the wife's heart is true and God will bless her and her home. And God will lead both husband and wife into ever-increasing blessedness together.

It will be this way between the believer and God. God will not always be pleased with the believer. The believer may grieve God every day, but he can be thankful for the faith in his soul that assures him God will never leave him or forsake him. God's patience is longsuffering. "But where sin abounded, grace did much more abound" (Rom. 5:20). When the believer allows anything to come between God and him, something happens to chill the soul. That is what Malachi is saying here.

> Ye have wearied the Lord with your words. Yet ye say,
> Wherein have we wearied him? When ye say, Every one that
> doeth evil is good in the sight of the Lord, and he delighteth in
> them; or Where is the God of judgment? (Mal. 2:17).

The prophet goes on in Malachi 3:7 to bring out the most important message: "Return unto me, and I will return unto you, saith the Lord of hosts." This is God's great plea to His people: "Come back to me." They should turn once more to the One they first put their faith in. "And I will return unto you." All the blessedness they received when they first became believers could be theirs in reality now through the years of experience. But the Jews responded, "Wherein shall we return?" They were always asking questions to throw off the burden of the message.

> Will a man rob God? Yet ye have robbed me. But ye say,
> Wherein have we robbed thee? In tithes and offerings (Mal.
> 3:8).

We can feel the impudence and the insolence of spirit that
prompted these questions. Malachi told the people that God
was not fooled by their questions. God looked down into their
hearts.

In this matter of robbing God, Malachi writes this marvelous passage:

> Bring ye all the tithes into the storehouse, that there may be
> meat in mine house, and prove me now herewith, saith the
> Lord of hosts, if I will not open you the windows of heaven, and
> pour you out a blessing, that there shall not be room enough to
> receive it (Mal. 3:10).

This truth is applicable not only in the matter of money, for it
has to do with all obedience to God. Offering the tithe is a
matter of obedience, but the believer has time, energy, personal witness, and his share in all the things that are going on.
The believer does his part. He obeys the Lord and finds out
that God will pour out such a blessing that he cannot even
contain it. This is God's promise.

After Malachi preached so soberly and sternly, things
moved toward the harvest time. The sickle was about to be
wielded to reap the harvest. God would deal with His people
in final terms. His judgment was coming. And all this had
profound effect.

> Then they that feared the Lord spake often one to another: and
> the Lord hearkened, and heard it, and a book of remembrance
> was written before him for them that feared the Lord, and that
> thought upon his name (Mal. 3:16).

In Ezekiel's time there was a similar situation. This situation
occurs whenever there is widespread sluggishness, when believers are slow to obey, when they have alibied and
rationalized so that they feel they do not have to respond.
They are comfortable even though they are not praying; they
feel good enough day by day, so they do not read the Bible.
They do not feel any great loss and thus do not come to the
church services. They have it all figured out so they are at
ease. And in that condition the whole program of God is

lagging, and souls are not being saved, and young people are not being helped. Sin is rampant, and it looks as if believers are helpless.

Ezekiel saw in his day that the leaders of Jerusalem had their hearts turned to idolatry. In the chambers of their imagery they were bowing down to natural forces. In those days Ezekiel saw people in his vision who sighed and cried because of the abomination. They were bothered because of the way God was ignored. God said to His great messenger, "Go down and put a mark on them. Mark them. Because when the day of judgment comes, it is not going to come on those folks. They are mine."

So God looks down today. He looks into every congregation and into every person who calls upon the name of the Lord. There are some hungry souls. There are some earnest, sincere people who know the Lord, who want to see His name magnified, would love to hear Him praised in public, who are hungry for spiritual worship. Among such believers there develops a strange sort of fellowship: it is almost underground. These believers have their prayer meetings in a common bond of fellowship. They do not make it too obvious, but they get great comfort from knowing there is one over there and there is one over here who really cares and really believes.

God takes note of all these people. God in heaven is keeping a special record. He takes note of the mother who wishes her children were closer to God; the wife who grieves for her husband to be closer to God. If any of us wish our church were a stronger church, if we wish the officers would really be spiritually minded, if we wish that the church members would really live consistent lives, if we long for the power of God in the pulpit and in the pew of our congregation, and if we even ask God one time, He makes a record of it.

He knows us; He has His eyes on us. And God makes this promise:

> And they shall be mine, saith the Lord of hosts, in that day when I make up my jewels; and I will spare them, as a man spareth his own son that serveth him (Mal. 3:17).

God has His eye on the sincere believer. That believer belongs to Him. When a believer sighs and cries because of the abomination around about him, almighty God listens with great care. It is a sweet sound in His ears, because that believer cares. He wanted something better and he qualifies for God's close personal attention.

God has this believer in mind as surely as he lives and cares and weeps and longs for and prays and works and serves, in spite of so much discouragement, longsuffering, and long-deferred blessing.

The sincere believer waits and waits and waits; and he gives and gives; and nothing seems to come. He tries and tries, and nothing seems to happen. He prays and prays, and things do not seem to change. But all the time he is doing that, God Almighty has His eye on him. God has a book of remembrance about him.

We can recall a precious truth from the New Testament: the Lord Himself will come and walk with the sincere believer in the person of the Holy Spirit. That believer will have the Lord with him. The true believer does not need to walk alone. He may feel alone in this world, but if he knows the Lord, he is never alone. He walks with the Lord, and he suffers with Him. That believer will also reign with Him.

Just as surely as Malachi was the last prophet, and just as surely as we are moving toward the last days, just as surely as time will run its course, almighty God will move. When God moves, true believers will be brought into glory—into the glory of God. Our God is Savior and Lord and Father to all of us who believe.